Managing Conta
Young People

Managing Contact
for Young People

Sally Scott

Open University Press

Open University Press
McGraw-Hill Education
McGraw-Hill House
Shoppenhangers Road
Maidenhead
Berkshire
England
SL6 2QL

email: enquiries@openup.co.uk
world wide web: www.openup.co.uk

and Two Penn Plaza, New York, NY 10121–2289, USA

First published 2013

Copyright © Sally Scott, 2013

A catalogue record of this book is available from the British Library

ISBN-13: 978-0-33-524523-9 (pb)
ISBN-10: 0-33-524523-4 (pb)
eISBN: 978-0-33-526261-8

Library of Congress Cataloging-in-Publication Data
CIP data applied for

Typesetting and e-book compilations by
RefineCatch Limited, Bungay, Suffolk

Fictitious names of companies, products, people, characters and/or data that may be used herein
(in case studies or in examples) are not intended to represent any real individual, company,
product or event.

For Michael and Ben

Contents

How to use this book

This pocketbook is a practical guide to help workers to set up and manage contact for young people who are looked after. It is not written as an academic text but aims to reflect the everyday issues faced by workers and draws upon the policies and procedures of various statutory and voluntary agencies.

The book consists of eight chapters. These take you through the process of setting up and managing contact for young people who are looked after. Here is an overview of the book:

- Chapter 1 looks at the nuts and bolts of a contact arrangement. It gives a brief overview of the legal framework, explains some commonly used terms and considers why contact is necessary for young people who are looked after.
- Chapter 2 explains who is involved in contact arrangements and includes points to consider when working with children, families and other professionals.
- Chapter 3 goes through the process of assessing young people's needs in relation to contact and shows why individual contact arrangements should reflect the overall aim of a young person's care plan.
- Chapter 4 includes points to consider in relation to when and where to have contact.
- Chapter 5 looks at drawing up direct and indirect contact agreements for young people who are looked after.
- Chapter 6 looks at practical ways of managing direct and indirect arrangements.

- Chapter 7 discusses the important task of evaluation.
- Finally, Chapter 8 considers ways of recording contact.

This small pocketbook is designed to help you avoid the common pitfalls that workers encounter when setting up and managing contact. It includes checklists, reminders and examples of good practice for quick reference. Further reading and resources are included at the end of the book. You should use these to maintain and develop your practice.

Acknowledgements

I would like to thank the young people, their families and colleagues I have worked alongside in Yorkshire and County Limerick for sharing their experiences and views about contact. I am also grateful to my friends, family and colleagues at Huddersfield University for their support, advice and good humour.

Introduction

Most young people's contact with their friends and family is unplanned and happens informally, for example, through phone calls, texting or simply by living in the same house or attending the same school. However, for some young people, their circumstances are such that the relationship ties are complicated by the fact that they have been taken into care by the local authority, for whatever reason. In this case, the young person becomes 'looked after' by the local authority that has a responsibility to ensure that the young people maintain their relationships with significant people in their lives. This often means that more formal contact arrangements have to be made. This book is a guide for workers who are involved with making and supervising these formal contact arrangements.

In 2011, just under 90,000 young people were in the care of local authorities across the United Kingdom (BAAF 2011) and in order to maintain these relationships, workers from a variety of agencies are engaged with children and their families in setting up and managing contact arrangements.

All contact arrangements for young people who are looked after must do the following:

- They must meet statutory obligations set out in Acts of Parliament. We shall discuss these in later chapters.
- They must fit with the overall aims of their care plan.
- They must conform to the policies and procedures of the relevant agency.

This can be a complex process and it is not surprising that workers often feel ill prepared to tackle this task, and that lessons are often learned through trial and error.

This book will help you to manage successful contact arrangements for your service users of all ages and for whatever reason they are in care.

1 The nuts and bolts of contact

This first chapter will help you to understand what contact is and why it happens. It includes a brief overview of the legal framework and explanations of some commonly used terms. 'Contact' is used to refer to a whole variety of ways in which young people can maintain significant relationships when they are looked after by the local authority.

WHAT IS CORPORATE PARENTING?

Agencies often talk about 'corporate parenting'. This term has no formal legal definition and was introduced following the launch of the Quality Protects programme (Department of Health 1998) which aimed to improve the outcomes for children and young people who were in need, particularly those who were looked after by local authorities.

The concept acknowledges that children's services do not have *sole* responsibility for looked after children and encourages all members and officers of the council to be concerned about each looked-after child as if they were their own. However, in practice, it is the legal responsibility of the social worker for the young person to act as the corporate parent on day-to-day matters. This includes setting up and managing the contact arrangements.

**Good Practice Point:
Corporate Parenting**

As the corporate parent responsible for setting up contact arrangements it may be helpful to ask yourself: If this was my child, would this be good enough for them, would it be good enough for me? (Stein 2009: 13).

CONTACT ARRANGEMENTS IN PRIVATE AND PUBLIC LAW

Contact arrangements for children can be dealt with as a matter of either 'private' and/or 'public' law. The majority of contact arrangements for young people are made between individuals in 'private law matters' and will not involve social workers. For example, divorcing parents who cannot agree about arrangements for their children may make an application for a contact order in private law. In contrast, 'public law' provides a mechanism for the state to protect children by intervening in a family's life. This usually involves social workers. For example, if a local authority has concerns about the safety of a child, it may make an application for a care order or a contact order in public law. It is worth remembering that, contact arrangements that start as 'private law matters' can end up as 'public law matters'. For example, if a court dealing with a contact dispute in private law has concerns about one of the parents, it can decide to involve the local authority, who may go on to make an application for a care order under public law.

THE IMPACT OF PRIMARY, SECONDARY LEGISLATION AND CASE LAW

The Children Act 1989 and the Children and Young Persons Act 2008 are the key pieces of primary legislation that outline the duties that local authorities have in relation to the contact arrangements for young people who are looked after. A key principle of the 1989 Act is that children are best looked after within their families. For children who are looked after *outside* their families, the legislation encourages parents to continue to play a part in their child's life wherever possible. The Children Act 1989 identifies contact as a right of the child (in other words, parents, relatives and others do not have a 'right' to contact). However, local authorities have a legal duty to provide and promote contact, unless it is not in the best interests of the child.

Regulations, known as 'secondary legislation', also impact upon contact arrangements. Secondary legislation, such as the Care Planning, Placement and Case Review (England) Regulations 2010 are made under specific powers under a piece of legislation. They contain legal requirements and have the same status as legislation.

The different interpretations of legislation relating to contact arrangements in both public law and private law can be found in case law. Case law can set legal precedent, but it can also be overturned.

 Point of Law: Parental Responsibility

Parental responsibility (often known as 'PR') is defined as 'all the rights, duties, powers, responsibilities and authority which by law a parent of a child has in relation to a child and his/her property' (Children Act 1989, Section 3(1)).

In other words, those with parental responsibility have the power to make decisions relating to the everyday upbringing of the child in relation to things like medical treatment, where the child will live, which school they attend and who they have contact with.

Making a care order gives parental responsibility to the local authority but it does not *totally* remove parental responsibility from the parents. When negotiating contact arrangements it is important to acknowledge both the rights and responsibilities of birth parents. However, when you are setting up the arrangements it is important to remember that contact is the right of the child, *not* the parent.

'IN CARE' AND 'LOOKED AFTER'

This book focuses upon contact arrangements in public law. It relates specifically to young people who are 'in care' or 'looked after children' (sometimes this is abbreviated to 'LAC'). It does not look specifically at contact arrangements for young people who are (or about to be) adopted.

The terms 'in care' and 'looked after' are often used interchangeably though they are different. The only way for a child to be 'in care' is by a court granting a care order. So, if there is no care order, then the child is not 'in care'. Young people are 'in care' if they are subject to the following:

- care orders;
- interim care orders.

Point of Law: The No Order Principle

The court will only make an order (such as a care order or contact order) when it considers it would be better for the child to do so rather than making no order at all. This is known as the 'no order principle'.

The term 'looked after' is much broader than the term 'in care'. It includes young people who are subject to care orders and interim care orders and also those who are subject to the following restrictions:

- under Emergency Protection Orders;
- 'accommodated' under Section 20 of the Children Act 1989;
- placed (or authorized to be placed) for adoption;
- subject to court order with a residence requirement, such as young people on secure remand to local authority accommodation.

CONTACT ORDERS

Put simply, a contact order spells out who will have contact with a young person. It says how often the contact will be and how long it will be for. Some of the young people you are working with will be subject to contact orders, others will not. You may be involved in making an application for a contact order. For example, when a special guardianship order is granted, it is expected that the young person will maintain links with their parents so the court will also consider the need to make a contact order.

THE PARAMOUNCY PRINCIPLE AND THE WELFARE CHECKLIST

There is no standard 'pro forma' for contact orders, however, in making any decision in relation to looked after children, including decisions about contact, the welfare of the child is the court's paramount consideration. This is known as the paramouncy principle.

The court will also consider the 'welfare checklist' when making decisions. This is defined in Section 1(3) of the Children Act 1989.

Good Practice Checklist: The Welfare Checklist

The welfare checklist includes:

✓ the wishes and feelings of the child;
✓ the child's physical, emotional and educational needs;
✓ the likely effect on the child of any change in circumstances;
✓ the child's age, sex, background and any other characteristics which the court considers relevant;
✓ any harm which the child has suffered or is at risk of suffering;
✓ how capable each parent, or any other relevant person, is of meeting the child's needs.

Contact orders commonly determine the contact arrangements between parents and their children. They may also apply to arrangements for contact between siblings or the child and other family members. Orders last until the child is 16 years old, although the court can make contact orders in relation to children aged over 16 in exceptional circumstances. Some orders are very specific, for example, they can apply to particular periods of time or give directions relating to supervision, while other orders are more open to allow the parties to agree the details.

A contact order made by the courts is legally binding. This means that the people with whom the child lives must allow that child to have contact with the people named in the order, and failure to comply with these arrangements can result in the court making further orders. However, granting a contact order does not necessarily result in people working together collaboratively. In practice, people are more likely to 'buy into' contact arrangements that are reached through negotiation than those imposed by the court.

LEGAL STATUS AND CONTACT ARRANGEMENTS

It is important to determine the legal status of the young person as this will impact upon the contact arrangements. Table 1.1 shows the contact arrangements for young people who are subject to care orders because of their different circumstances.

 Point of Law: Placement with Parents (PWP)

In some cases, young people subject to a care order or an interim care order can be placed at home with their parent(s) (PWP) in accordance with specific regulations (known as the Care Planning, Placement and Case Review (England) Regulations 2010).

In 2011, 6 per cent of the young people looked after in England were placed with their parents. In most cases, the parents have the day-to-day responsibility for the care of the child and will make their own contact arrangements although a social worker may be involved in some situations, for example, if the parents are living separately.

These regulations are also used when a young person subject to a care order is planning to spend a period of more than 24 hours in the care of a parent.

Types of Contact

In practice, you will come across various plans for contact. These show how much arrangements have changed over the years. Findings from research, emerging theories of child development and the introduction of new guidance and legislation have all impacted upon the attitudes, practices and language relating to contact.

Table 1.1 Contact arrangements for young people subject to care orders

The majority of contact arrangements are made in relation to young people who are subject to care orders.

Care orders are only granted by the court where it has been demonstrated that a child is at risk of significant harm.

The effect of care orders, interim care orders and emergency care orders is to give the local authority effective parental responsibility for a child. This means that the local authority can make decisions about the child 'in loco parentis' (in the place of the parent).

The factors that lead to the care proceedings will impact upon the contact arrangements for that child and family. This may affect type of contact and levels of supervision.

Contact arrangements for young people who are 'accommodated'

Unlike a care order, accommodation is a voluntary arrangement between those with parental responsibility and the local authority.

Parents of young people who are accommodated under Section 20 of the Children Act 1989 retain parental responsibility for their child.

Accommodated young people are 'looked after' but there is no care order, so they are not 'in care'.

Those with parental responsibility can withdraw their consent and have contact with their child at any time.

If contact arrangements cannot be successfully negotiated, then you may consider making an application for a contact order.

Contact arrangements for young people under police protection

In very exceptional cases, you may be involved in contact arrangements for young people under police protection.

This is not an order granted by a court. Therefore, it should *not* be referred to as a police protection order.

When a child is placed in police protection, the police do not acquire parental responsibility but the designated officer for that child is responsible for allowing whatever contact is felt to be in the child's best interest.

If a child under police protection is removed to accommodation provided by the local authority, then the local authority is responsible for managing the contact arrangements.

Contact arrangements for young people in secure accommodation

A very small number of young people are subject to a secure accommodation order.

These young people are considered to be 'looked after' if the local authority is funding the cost of the secure placement.

Young people are not considered to be 'looked after' if they are sentenced to reside in secure accommodation due to their offending behaviour and the cost of the placement is funded by the Home Office.

Contact arrangements for young people who are adopted

The effect of an adoption order is to grant parental responsibility to the adoptive parents.

Adoptive parents have the same legal position as birth parents and assume responsibility for arranging contact for their child.

In practice, you may still be involved in arrangements with adopted children, for example, if you are working with a looked-after sibling of an adopted child.

Contact arrangements for young people under Special Guardianship Orders (SGO)

A Special Guardianship Order (known as an SGO) is a private law order which appoints an individual to be a young person's special guardian.

SGOs are relatively new. They are used in cases where young people cannot live with their parents but need a secure placement.

(Continued overleaf)

Table 1.1 (Continued)

A SGO is more secure than a residence order but less permanent than placing a child for adoption.

A SGO does not end the legal relationship between the child and the birth parents, who retain limited PR. However, it does confer PR on the special guardian. This means that the special guardians can make day-to-day decisions relating to the care and upbringing of the child.

Young people subject to SGOs can live outside the UK for up to three months. This may have implications for contact arrangements.

Generally, children who are subject to SGOs remain in contact with their family as long as it is in their best interest to do so.

Legislation also gives the local authority powers to support special guardianship arrangements. Therefore look at the terms of the order to see if anything has been agreed in relation to contact arrangements.

Table 1.2 explains some of the various types of contact and the terms that are commonly used to describe them.

WHY IS CONTACT NECESSARY?

Now we have looked at the background and some of the key terms, we can go on to look at the reasons for contact.

Complying with Statutory Responsibilities

As we have seen, local authorities assume the role of corporate parents in relation to young people who are looked after. Their key responsibilities in relation to contact are outlined in primary and secondary legislation.

Table 1.2   Various types of contact

Type of contact	Explanation	Example
Direct	Face-to-face meetings where people are physically in the same place	A birthday party at the parent's house Young person sharing a meal with their siblings in a residential unit
Indirect	Communication is not face-to-face but uses another medium	A telephone call or text or email A school report or newsletter A DVD or audiotape
	Indirect contact can be one-way, for example, where the child contacts the parent, or two-way, where child and parent contact each other Indirect contact can supplement direct contact	A message via a social networking site A drawing or photograph A greetings card or gift
Supervised	Where there are concerns that a child may be at risk during the contact session, it may be supervised by a third party There are different levels of supervision. From constant observation through to less active participation or intermittent supervision	Mum has contact with child at contact centre. Contact worker provides constant supervision and stays within hearing distance at all times Social worker reads birthday cards and opens presents from family before passing them on to the young person

(Continued overleaf)

Table 1.2 (Continued)

Type of contact	Explanation	Example
	Direct and indirect contact can be supervised Supervisors can include social workers, contact staff, residential workers, foster carers and extended family	Siblings have contact with Dad at Aunt's home. Aunt goes into room to check everything is OK every ten minutes
Assessed	The contact session is observed and recorded within a structured assessment format	Guardian ad Litem completes parenting assessment of a couple and their baby in preparation for care proceedings
Unsupervised	Contact which is not supervised by a third party	Young person arranges to go to cinema with mum and step-dad
	Unsupervised contact may still need to be co-ordinated by third party	Social worker organizes shopping trip for teenager and her Aunt
Supported/facilitated	Contact that is supported or facilitated by third person to ensure that the needs of the children are met	Large family contact between mother and five young children is held at home of maternal grandmother who helps Mum to play with children

	Support should be only necessary to ensure the child's well-being	Contact worker assists social worker at start and end of contact session
	Support can be in relation to specific tasks, for example, transport, interpreting	
Phased	Contact arrangements that are planned to increase or decrease in frequency or length	Young person goes to the house of prospective foster carers before a placement starts. The first visit is for an hour, the second and third visits are for three hours at mealtimes, the fourth visit is all day, the fifth visit is overnight
Direct intervention	Contact sessions are used to engage with family in order to directly influence behaviour	Mum and toddlers go to parenting programme at children's centre
	Where the intervention is also being assessed, these two functions must remain distinct	
Structured	Contact that has a specific aim	Child completes a life story book with his Dad
Activity-based	Contact that is centred around a specific activity	Foster carers supervise monthly sibling contact at swimming pool

(Continued overleaf)

Table 1.2 (Continued)

Type of contact	Explanation	Example
Final/ goodbye/ farewell/ wishing you well	Last contact that takes place before child moves to adoptive family	Supervised meal at family centre
Holiday	Contact that occurs during school holidays or to celebrate religious festival	All-day contact at family home to celebrate Eid Weekend visit to siblings living in another foster placement
Letterbox	Contact service that co-ordinates the exchange of materials, for example, letters, photographs, via a third party. Usually used after adoption In cases where there is currently no contact, 'non-operational' letterboxes can be set up which may be activated later	An adopted child sends a card to the letterbox co-ordinator which is read and then forwarded to his birth mother
Extended	Contact that can be for long periods of time	Overnight home visits in preparation for accommodated young person to return to live with parents

Point of Law: The Presumption of Reasonable Contact

Section 34 of the Children Act 1989 says that local authorities must allow a young person to have *reasonable contact* unless the court gives the local authority permission to refuse it. This is known as the 'presumption of reasonable contact'. It relates to contact with parents, a guardian and/or special guardian, anyone with a residence order made immediately before the care order and step-parents who have parental responsibility.

There is no statutory definition of what constitutes 'reasonable' contact but it is clear that local authorities have a duty to promote reasonable contact *unless* it is detrimental to the child's welfare.

The local authority has a duty to promote reasonable contact as long as the child remains looked after *except* in exceptional cases, for example, where the local authority is granted authority to place a child for adoption. In this case, there is no presumption either for or against contact.

Point of Law: Promoting Contact

Schedule 2, paragraph 15(1) of the Children Act 1989 says that the local authority must endeavour to *promote contact* unless it is not reasonably practicable or not consistent with the young person's welfare. This relates to contact with parents, any person who has parental responsibility, any relative, friend or other person connected with the young person.

Put simply, the law says that arrangements should be made to promote reasonable contact unless it is not in the interests of the young person to do so.

Contact arrangements should also comply with statutory regulations and standards.

Good Practice Checklist:
The Care Planning, Placement and Case Review (England) Regulations 2010

✓ The Care Planning, Placement and Case Review (England) 2010 Regulations came into force in April 2011 and consolidate the existing regulations and guidance about care planning and review into one framework.

✓ The Regulations include detailed information in relation to contact. They consider who should be included in contact and look at different types of contact arrangements such as sibling contact.

✓ The underlying aim of contact is outlined in the accompanying 2010 care planning guidance (DCSF 2010). This guidance is part of a suite of statutory guidance which, together with the 2010 Regulations, sets out how local authorities should carry out the full range of responsibilities in relation to care planning, placement and review for looked-after children.

✓ This guidance states that contact arrangements should maintain the continuity of relationships and sustain significant attachments for looked-after children. It notes that parents should be expected and enabled to retain their parental responsibilities when their child cannot live at home either temporarily or permanently.

✓ Note: The 2010 Regulations *do not apply* in relation to any child who is looked after by a local authority and who has been placed for adoption under the Adoption and Children Act 2002.

As many looked-after children are placed in foster care, workers should also be aware of the standards relating to fostering services, i.e. the National Minimum Standards for Fostering Services and the UK National Standards for Foster Care.

Good Practice Checklist: National Minimum Standards for Fostering Services

✓ The National Minimum Standards for Fostering Services apply to all local authority fostering services, independent fostering agencies, and voluntary organizations providing fostering services.
✓ The regulations are mandatory and the standards are 'minimum' standards, rather than 'best possible' practice.
✓ Standard 10 is concerned with promoting contact for looked-after children.

Good Practice Checklist: The UK National Standards for Foster Care

✓ The UK National Standards for Foster Care were produced in 1999, along with the Code of Practices relating to foster carers.
✓ The National Standards cover all aspects of the life of the foster child, not just the services provided by fostering services.
✓ Unlike the National Minimum Standards, the National Standards have no formal legal status.
✓ The UK National Standards represent best practice and continue to be applicable to fostering services.

2 Deciding who to involve

As we have seen, statutory responsibilities shape the contact arrangements for all young people who are looked after. This chapter looks at who is involved in the contact arrangements and includes points to consider when working with children, families and other professionals.

Reminder Box: Focus on the Needs of the Child

As we have seen, local authorities have a duty to promote contact for looked-after children. In practice, this requires you to balance the competing needs of the child, their carers, their family and the agency. Although you should remain focused on the needs of the child, it is easy to become sidetracked, for example, by getting embroiled in negotiations between separated parents. Remember that in all decisions relating to looked-after children, the needs of the child are paramount and this should be the primary focus of the contact arrangements.

CONTACT WITH PARENTS AND THOSE WITH PARENTAL RESPONSIBILITY

The process of applying for a care order is adversarial and can create conflict between workers and those with parental responsibility for the child. This perception of 'them and us' may continue long after proceedings are concluded. It is understandable that it may take a long time for parents to come to terms with losing the day-to-day responsibilities of caring for their child and those parents who have relinquished their parenting role may now feel that they have nothing to offer their children through contact. Although the needs of the child are paramount, the contact arrangements should take into account the wishes and feelings of parents and carers wherever possible.

- Looked-after children may have contact with any person who has parental responsibility. So check who has parental responsibility for the child. It may well be a father who is not married to the mother of the child.
- When negotiating contact arrangements, it is important to overcome stereotypes and engage with *both* parents, including those who may be living outside the former family home.
- A child's parents may have separated and/or have formed new relationships since the children were received into care. In this case, it is important to talk to parents and step-parents separately and acknowledge they may have very different views and attitudes in relation to contact.
- If the parents were also 'looked-after children' themselves, they will bring their own experiences of contact and/or may feel a sense of history repeating itself.
- While many parents feel guilt or grief about no longer looking after their child, they may also fear that if contact goes well they will be expected to resume the full-time care of their child.
- Check the reason for a child losing contact with a parent. For example, contact may have ceased when a child was placed for adoption and may not have been re-established if the adoption subsequently broke down.
- If re-establishing contact, ensure that it focuses on the needs of the child.

> ### Example from Practice: Focus on the Needs of the Child
>
> When Millie was 7, her Mum, Fiona, went on holiday, leaving her daughter in the care of a friend. When Fiona failed to return, Millie was received into the care of the local authority and placed with foster parents. Two years later, Fiona phoned the social worker to say that she had returned to the UK and had the right to see her daughter immediately. Rather than arranging contact, the social worker arranged to meet with Fiona in order to assess the current situation before considering any plans for contact.

CONTACT WITH SIBLINGS

> Our contact with our siblings are the longest in our lives, and we must not risk that children who are already losing much, should lose more.
>
> (Argent 1995: 67)

It is good practice to place brothers and sisters together wherever possible. If siblings are placed separately in the short term, the level of contact between them needs to be high enough to maintain their relationship in order for them to be placed together in the future. If it is decided to place siblings in separate long-term placements, it is important to facilitate and support the ongoing contact arrangements between them.

> ### Point of Law: Children Act Regulations 2010
>
> Schedule 1, Paragraph 3(1) of the Children Act Regulations 2010 says that a young person's care plan must set out the arrangements for them to maintain contact with any siblings who are also looked after but placed separately.

Ideally, siblings will be allocated the same social worker, but when this is not the case, workers need to liaise with the parents, carers and the social work colleagues to plan ahead and reduce the duplication of work. It is important to work together from the start as once patterns of contact become established, they can be difficult to change.

Relationships between many brothers and sisters can be complex. It is particularly important to consider the family dynamics when siblings have shared experience of abuse and neglect within their family and it may be necessary to make further assessments in order to inform the contact arrangements:

- Young people will have different memories and understandings about their family. This will affect their hopes and fears in relation to contact, for example, a child who 'blew the whistle' on abuse at home may fear they will be blamed for splitting up the family whereas another child who was subject to abuse may feel anxious about being adequately protected during contact.
- Contact can also help to alleviate fears, for example, visiting a sibling in their placement may enable a child to be reassured that they are safe and well cared for.
- The roles siblings had in the family may also affect their behaviour during contact, for example, children may assume a parental or protective role or demonstrate sexualized and/or aggressive behaviour.
- Marked differences between the siblings' placements may create jealousy or rivalry in contact, for example, if one child is placed with an affluent family and another is not, or if one child is in a temporary placement, while their sibling has been found an adoptive family.
- The age and interests of the child will determine the type of contact that they want and can cope with, for example, some young people may enjoy revisiting the past by looking at

photographs or doing life story work, others may prefer
something more active.

■ Think about who is involved in facilitating contact and be aware
that young people may have 'split loyalties', for example, between
their birth family and the current carers.

■ Be realistic about the proposed contact arrangements. Social
networking sites and mobile phones are easily accessible so it
may be more practical to manage indirect contact than try to
prevent it.

CONTACT WITH EXTENDED FAMILY AND FRIENDS

When young people are living apart from their birth parents, contact
with friends and members of the extended family can help to maintain
cultural ties and family history that can easily be lost:

■ Young people's relationships with non-family members, such as
teachers, neighbours or youth workers, can often be lost when
they become looked after and it may beneficial to maintain
contact with these significant people.

■ Extended family and friends can often view contact arrangements
more objectively than parents. They can act as effective
intermediaries in order to broker contact arrangements. However,
having divided loyalties may make them unsuitable for this role.

■ Bear in mind that friends and family members may be reluctant
to engage in contact arrangements for fear that they will be
approached to assume the full-time caring role for the young
person.

■ Play to people's strengths, for example, in direct contact
arrangements, people may assist with tasks such as providing a
venue, transport or support. Where contact is indirect, they may
help with writing letters, sending photos or making phone calls.

CONTACT WITH KNOWN PERPETRATORS

Children have the right to enjoy regular contact with both parents and family members provided that it is safe for them to do so. In some circumstances, this will involve managing contact with known perpetrators of child abuse and/or domestic violence:

- Ask about the perpetrator's current motivation to see the young person.
- Get information about the nature of previous offences and the perpetrator's previous *modus operandi*.
- Check whether there is an ongoing police investigation that may affect or be affected by the contact arrangements.
- Liaise with your manager and colleagues from other agencies, such as probation services and the police, in order to assess whether direct or indirect contact is likely to pose a threat to the child or to others.

WORKING WITH OTHER PROFESSIONALS

Setting up contact arrangements requires effective liaison with other colleagues across a number of agencies. This section includes points to consider when you are working with other professionals involved in contact for looked-after children.

Social Workers

Each looked-after child has a named social worker who is responsible for setting up and managing the contact arrangements.

- Some contact arrangements may require liaison between social workers from different statutory teams. For example, arranging a family contact visit may involve workers from children and adult services from different local authorities. It may also involve social workers from non-statutory agencies, such as private fostering agencies or contact teams.

■ It is preferable to maintain continuity and minimize the number of people involved in facilitating the contact arrangements.

■ If contact has to be facilitated by a colleague or duty worker at short notice, ensure that the child and all other parties are notified of the change in advance and that the worker 'covering' the contact is familiar with the contact plan and is aware of any known risks and the safeguards that are in place.

Contact Workers

Some local authorities and agencies do their own contact work. Others have an 'in-house' contact team who manage all or part of the contact arrangements. Some organizations 'contract out' contact work to voluntary or private agencies.

■ Check your agency's policies and procedures to ensure you understand the roles and responsibilities of each agency.

■ If other agencies are involved in the contact arrangements, make sure to liaise with them *well before* the contact arrangements are finalized to ensure that you are both clear about your joint remit, and procedures for communicating and recording the contact.

Foster Carers

Foster carers are contracted to provide the day-to-day care for looked-after children within the fostering regulations. Foster carers are supported by link workers, either from the local authority's family placement team or a private agency.

■ Many foster carers will have detailed understanding of the child's routines and preferences and this can be very helpful in relation to planning and supporting contact arrangements.

■ Foster carers work in their own homes and adequate safeguards need to be in place to support them with the contact arrangements. It can be helpful to meet with foster carers and their link worker to ensure that the arrangements are workable, that they 'fit' with the child's and carer's commitments and take into account the needs of any other children in the house.

■ Once the contact arrangements are in place, it is useful to review these informally with the carers and the link worker and deal with problems as you go along than rather than wait for a crisis.

■ In order to support the contact arrangements, foster carers may benefit from additional information or training, for example, information about the child's family background, domestic violence or patterns of attachment.

Relative Carers

Some looked-after children are placed with relatives, for example, under a Special Guardianship Order. When young people live in this type of 'kinship care', contact often occurs informally. While this has many benefits, it may make the arrangements more difficult to monitor.

■ In most cases, relative carers have been approved to care for a particular child and do not necessarily see themselves as 'foster carers' for the local authority.

■ Relative carers may collude with some family members or be reluctant to facilitate contact with others. They may need additional support to promote contact that is beneficial to the child.

Good Practice Point: Supporting the Relationship Between Carers and Parents

Good communication between you, the family and the carers will help the contact arrangements to run more smoothly and it is helpful to support this relationship wherever possible.

Meeting their child's carers, either in placement or at a neutral venue, before the contact arrangements are finalized can enable parents to see who their child is living with. It provides them with an opportunity to share information about their child's likes and dislikes, their routines and their medical history. This can give parents a sense of doing something valuable for their child and may give the child 'permission' to accept their new placement.

'Standing in the shoes' of parents and carers may help you to anticipate problems and provide support. For example, a birth parent may see themselves as 'incapable' as opposed to the 'capable' alternative carers or foster carers. The carers who are opposed to rehabilitating a child home may criticize parents in an attempt to undermine this plan.

Residential Workers

With adequate negotiation and support, residential workers can play a central role in planning and facilitating contact arrangements. It makes sense to work closely with residential staff from the outset in order to make the most of what residential units can offer to support contact arrangements.

■   Many units are open and staffed around the clock. They generally have access to cooking facilities, are available free of charge and may have a budget for activities! Residential workers may support and facilitate contact arrangements in a number of ways, for example, by providing transport, helping the young person prepare a meal for their family or supervising a visit.

- Residential staff, in particular, the young person's key worker, will be familiar with their daily routine. They are likely to be aware of the young person's likes and dislikes and have experience of managing any challenging behaviour.
- When arranging direct contact at the unit, you should take into account the layout of the building, the levels of staffing and the need to maintain the privacy of the other young people. Remember, it is their home too.
- If contact is indirect, residential workers may advise and assist the child, for example, by helping them write letters, or make phone calls.

Independent Reviewing Officers (IROs)

An Independent Reviewing Officer, known as an 'IRO', is appointed for every looked-after child. It is the responsibility of the IRO to ensure that the wishes and feelings of the child are given due consideration by the local authority. IROs chair the 'statutory review' of the young person's care plan. This includes evaluating the contact arrangements.

- IROs are experienced workers who often have a great deal of historical information about the looked-after child and their family and can be a good source of advice and guidance. Workers may find it useful to discuss any proposed changes to the care plan and contact arrangements with the IRO between statutory reviews.
- Workers must consult with IROs in relation to significant events that impact upon the care of a looked-after child, such as the allocation of a new social worker or major changes to the care plan.

Independent Visitors

Occasionally, looked-after children have infrequent or no contact at all with their family or friends. In this case, you may consider appointing an independent person to visit:

- If you believe it is in a child's best interest, *and*
- the communication between the child and parent (or person with PR) has been infrequent, *or*
- The child has not seen his parents (or person with PR) during the preceding 12 months.
- The decision to appoint an independent visitor has to be made in consultation with the child. You should not appoint an independent visitor against a young person's wishes if you are satisfied that they have sufficient understanding to make an informed decision about it.

YOUR PART IN THE CONTACT ARRANGEMENT

Remember the impact of self! Our individual attitudes, motivations and fears affect the way we behave and how we are viewed by others. Figure 2.1 may help you to recognize how your emotions and

1	2
What is known by the person about him/herself and is also known by others	What is unknown by the person about him/herself but that is known by others
3	4
What the person knows about him/herself but that others do not know	What is unknown by the person about him/herself and is also unknown by others

Figure 2.1 The Johari window

behaviour impact upon the way you set up and manage contact. The model is based on Luft and Ingham's (1950) Johari Window concept. The whole window includes information about ourselves, for example, our feelings, emotions and motivations. This information can be located in one of four panes which show whether this information is known or unknown to us, and whether the information is known or unknown to others.

The size of each pane reflects the relevant proportions of each type of 'knowledge' about a particular person. For example, as a new worker in a team, it is likely that pane number 1 will be small because you are an 'unknown quantity'. However, as you become established and known by other members of the team, the size of this pane will increase.

Being aware of what you know about yourself and what others know about you will help you to manage and evaluate contact.

Good Practice Checklist: Deciding Who to Involve

✓ Identify *all* past and current significant relationships within and outside the family.
✓ Ascertain and manage people's hopes and fears about contact.
✓ Comply with statutory requirements.
✓ Focus on the needs of the young person.

3 Making an assessment

Chapter 2 looked at who is involved in the contact arrangements. This chapter explains how to make an assessment of young people's needs in relation to contact. It considers different approaches to care planning and shows why individual contact arrangements should reflect the overall aim of a young person's care plan.

MAKING ASSESSMENTS IN RELATION TO CONTACT

In order to plan the contact arrangements for a looked-after child, we need to find out what 'we know we know'. This is done by gathering and assessing information. This assessment will inform how, when and where contact should occur.

As the Donald Rumsfeld, the former US Secretary of Defense famously said:

> There are known knowns; there are things we know we know. We also know there are known unknowns; that is to say we know there are some things we do not know. But there are also unknown unknowns – the ones we don't know we don't know.
>
> (US Department of Defense 2002)

GATHERING INFORMATION

Assessments are based on an analysis of information. This can be gathered from a variety of sources. The two main ways of doing this are looking at the case file and talking to the people involved.

Documents in the Case File

The documents in the case file will contain key information that will help to inform the contact arrangements. Case files for looked-after children can contain hundreds of documents, and bear in mind that some local authorities use documents that are based on the templates developed by the Department of Health whereas other local authorities use their own 'in-house' versions.

Legal Documents

Care orders and contact orders will provide information about the reasons that children came into care and details of people who may and may not have contact. These are legal documents.

'Looked After' Documents

There may be other documents that are important to the case.

- *The core assessment*: This assessment should be completed prior to the young person becoming looked after. The purpose of a core assessment is to clarify and identify the needs of the child by gathering information from all the professionals working with a child and their family. In practice, local authorities may use their own versions of the core assessment and have different procedures to complete them. However, all assessments are based upon the seven dimensions of a child's developmental needs, as set out in the Framework for the Assessment of Children in Need and their Families (Department of Health 2000), and these should be taken into account when deciding on contact arrangements. The analysis of the information gathered in the core assessment forms the basis of the young person's care plan.
- *Assessment and progress record*: For children who remain looked after for longer periods, the information in the core assessment

may be supplemented by information in the assessment and
progress record.

■ *Care plans*: This key document identifies the overall plan for the
care of the child. Remember to look at both the current and
previous care plans. They will give historical context about the
parenting capacity of the birth family, the young person's legal
status and previous family and social relationships. Old care plans
may include details of family members, those who have parental
responsibility and other people who are significant to the child
(including those who may no longer have contact).

Good Practice Point: Aims and Objectives in the Care Plan

When you are reading the care plan, make sure you look at
the aims and objectives of the contact arrangements in order
to ensure they reflect the aim of the current care plan.
Having a clear understanding of these will help you to plan
future contact arrangements and evaluate progress when the
care plan is reviewed by the IRO at the next statutory
review.

The overarching care plan may include the following documents:

■ *The placement plan*: This identifies why the placement was chosen
and how it meets the young person's needs. It also gives
information about how a young person is cared for on a day-
to-day basis, including the contact arrangements and any
practical and financial supports that are in place.

■ *The permanence plan*: This sets out the long-term plan for
the young person. These plans aim to achieve permanency for
young people who are looked after. It is important that the

contact arrangements are 'in line' with the aims of the long-term plan.

■ *The pathway plan*: A pathway plan is in place until the young person is 21 years old (or 25 if they are in education). It outlines the actions which will enable the young person to make a successful transition from care and should take contact arrangements into account.

■ *The health plan*: This is a statement of the young person's health care needs and indicates how those needs will be addressed. This may contain information that could impact upon the contact arrangements, for example, if the young person has allergies, is prescribed medication or has a physical disability.

■ *The personal education plan*: Often referred to as the 'PEP', this is a summary of a young person's developmental and educational needs. The personal education plan includes the contact details of staff, such as class teachers or key workers at nursery, who may be involved in the contact arrangements.

Common Pitfall: 'Start Again Syndrome'

A social worker's propensity to be over-optimistic about their impact on a case is known as the 'start again syndrome'. This common pitfall has been highlighted in several Serious Case Reviews and is a particular danger for inexperienced workers who are keen to give everyone another chance to make contact work.

It is important to be aware of the 'start again syndrome' and to review case records and chronologies to identify trends and patterns of behaviour. This information can identify what has worked well and also highlight any problems that have been encountered in previous contact arrangements. Workers should discuss any significant proposed changes to the existing contact arrangements with their manager who may have a more objective view.

While the documents from the case file can provide a great deal of information, it is important to see them as a 'snapshot' that has been taken through the lens of the agency. In order to get a more recent and complete picture, information from the case file should be reviewed by talking with the people involved.

TALKING WITH THOSE INVOLVED IN CONTACT

In practice, it can be difficult to ascertain everyone's views about contact. Moves in placement, staff turnover and changes in birth family's circumstances can result in information being lost and young people losing contact with people who are significant in their lives.

Good Practice Point: Ascertaining the Views of Children and Families

Workers may find it helpful to use a variety of tools to help people to identify family and friends with whom they would like to maintain contact. Using toys and games or drawing relationships using family trees, genograms or ecomaps can be useful ways of representing complex family relationships. These tools can be helpful to overcome communication barriers such as illiteracy, sight impairments or learning difficulties. Additional information such as names, ages and significant family events can be added later if necessary.

> ### Example from Practice: Family Trees
>
> Sam is the social worker for Archie (aged 7) who was placed in long-term foster care. In order to find out more about the contact arrangements, Sam helped Archie map out a family tree using toy figures and photographs to represent the people involved in contact. This helped Sam get to know Archie and find out about his version of his family's structure and history.

It is important that children do not see the assessment process as a way of 'testing' their commitment to relationships. Avoid putting them in a position where they have to choose between people, and give them plenty of scope to change their mind about who they would like contact with. You may also need to remind children that all their wishes may not be possible. As the 'corporate parent', you have to assess what the young person is able to cope with and what is in their long-term best interest.

Bear in mind that families use different language to express their relationships and you may need to interpret these. Many children have significant relationships with people they call 'auntie' and 'uncle' though there is no blood tie.

For many young people, these 'uncles' and 'aunts' can be very significant in helping them to maintain their sense of cultural identity. It may be impossible for young people who are seeking asylum to have direct contact with immediate family members. However, you may be able to identify other non-related adults living in the UK who could have face-to-face contact with the child.

Genograms

Genograms are a more detailed version of a family tree and can be a good way of presenting visual information about current and previous relationships. Genograms can be particularly helpful in identifying the child's relationships with non-family members such as friends, neighbours, teachers or ex-carers. These may be significant attachments that can be maintained through contact.

Bear in mind that there are likely to be various interpretations regarding certain issues. For instance, a young person may tell you she has a very close connection with her brother, whereas he may view it as a distant relationship. The exercise may also identify forgotten relatives or friends with whom contact has been lost. In this case you need to consider the possibility of re-establishing contact. Genograms may also reveal unexpected relationships such as strong attachments to pets.

Ecomaps

Ecomaps show the interrelationships between family members. They also locate the family within wider society and can be used to show the family's relationships with professionals, such as schools and social workers. This may help to inform contact arrangements.

Using the right tool for the job can help to ascertain children's and adults' views, wishes and attitudes in relation to contact. The process of gathering information also gives you an opportunity to introduce yourself and explain your role. It also enables you to get up-to-date contact details for all parties and to check what is going on for people now, such as working arrangements, or current relationships.

Reminder Box:
Remain Open-minded

Bear in mind that the information-gathering process may reignite old concerns and fears. In many cases, particularly where there have been contested proceedings, it is common for the opposing parties to continue to make allegations and counter-allegations. It is important to listen to people's views but remember that the various people involved in contact arrangements may have very different agendas.

As you gather information, try to remain open-minded but do not unquestioningly accept all you are told. You may need to remind people that the information they are giving will be checked out and that specific concerns will be investigated if necessary.

Throughout your discussions it is important to bring the focus back to the contact arrangements. You must explain clearly that you will be making decisions about contact in the best interests of the child.

YOUNG PEOPLE'S DEVELOPMENTAL NEEDS AND UNDERSTANDING

Contact arrangements should reflect the developmental needs and understanding of each young person. A baby's early years are crucial for brain development and forming secure attachments (Glaser 2000), so, in practice, the frequency of contact with babies has to be gauged in order for it to be meaningful to a child without disrupting their relationships and routine.

Bear in mind that the type of contact arrangements will convey meaning about the future of the relationship between a child and their parents, so it is also important to check out the young person's understanding of the reasons behind the contact arrangements.

Young People with Additional Needs

Some young people may have views about contact which they cannot express verbally. When you are ascertaining views, think creatively about ways of ascertaining young people's views, for example, using drawings, model houses and people or photographs are simple ways for young people to communicate non-verbally.

If specialist help is required, such as with signing or translation, think about who is best placed to assist. Be aware that using carers or family members to ascertain the young person's views may compromise their ability to express their wishes openly.

Good Practice Checklist: Gathering Information

Reading the young person's case file and talking to those involved should have helped you to gather information. This may include the following kinds of information:

The Legal Position

✓ the legal status of each young person;
✓ details of those with parental responsibility;
✓ details of any court orders.

Requirements of Your Agency

✓ the agency's policies and procedures in relation to contact;
✓ recommendations from the last statutory review.

The Needs of the Child

✓ the young person's age and development;
✓ health, dietary or medical issues;
✓ emotional and/or behavioural difficulties;
✓ cultural identity.

The Current Contact Arrangements

✓ the overall aim of the child's care plan;
✓ the current contact agreement and the date it was last reviewed;

✓ the rationale behind the current contact arrangements;
✓ the roles and responsibilities of those involved;
✓ the details of supports that are in place;
✓ the method of communicating and recording the contact arrangements;
✓ full contact details of individuals and agencies involved.

Participants' Approach to Contact

✓ expectations and wishes in relation to contact;
✓ details of any history or threat of abuse to the child, other carers or staff;
✓ attitude to assisting with future contact arrangements.

Considerations in Relation to Venue and Transport

✓ physical and medical needs of participants;
✓ cultural or religious requirements;
✓ transport links and travelling times.

Considerations in Relation to Timetabling Contact

✓ carers', parents' and young people's commitments;
✓ social or religious dates and events;
✓ contact arrangements for other siblings.

Resources Required

✓ the time and costs involved;
✓ the need for additional support.

ASSESSING THE INFORMATION

Once you have gathered the information, the next step is to assess it. In the same way as you solve a mathematical problem, the assessment process is about 'showing your workings' and the reasons for particular contact arrangements should be supported by evidence. Adopting an evidence-based approach will also help you to explain the reasons for your decisions to others, for example, to the child, the IRO or the court.

From your studies you may have knowledge of current theories and research findings in relation to contact arrangements. As you gain experience of managing contact arrangements, you will become more confident about relating this knowledge to practice in order to make evidence-based assessments.

Assessing and Managing Risk

Assessing risk is one element of the contact planning process. Like other aspects of the assessment, it can only be based on the information you have gathered.

If we think back to Mr Rumsfeld's remark, there will always be 'unknown unknowns'. In other words, it is not possible to eradicate risk entirely but it is possible to manage it. Once you have identified the possible hazards, you can put safeguards in place to decrease the likelihood of the risk happening and/or reduce the severity of its impact.

Good liaison with other agencies, carers and family members can enable you to anticipate and manage significant risks. Multi-Agency Public Protection Arrangements (known as 'MAPPA meetings') are used to assess and manage the risk posed by sexual and violent offenders. These can provide you with information about the treatment and release date of prisoners. It may also assist in the provision and co-ordination of safeguards such as intruder alarms and security locks.

Risk assessments should also take into account levels of vulnerability, for example, babies and young people with disabilities may be particularly vulnerable to abuse. When setting up direct contact, think through the practicalities of the proposed arrangements, for example, in relation to feeding and managing personal care, to ensure that they incorporate adequate safeguards and levels of supervision.

Common Pitfalls: Failing to Review the Risk Assessment

In the same way that we continually re-assess the risk of being hit by an oncoming car as we cross the road, it is important that we review our risk assessments in relation to contact arrangements. In practice, contact arrangements tend to remain the same even though the level of risk may have changed, for example, as a young person grows older and more able to manage independently, the level of supervision required is likely to decrease.

As you gain experience of managing contact arrangements in practice, you will observe that the thresholds of acceptable risk are influenced by the culture of the agency and the tolerance of individual workers. Some will be more risk-averse than others! Try and remain open-minded and use opportunities such as supervision sessions to question and evaluate your assessments.

It is important that the assessment also takes into account the overall aim of the young person's care plan.

Care Planning and Contact

Every looked-after child must have a care plan. These provide a 'roadmap' for each young person's journey through care and the purpose of contact should reflect the overall aim of the care plan. If the overall aim is to rehabilitate a child home, then the purpose of contact may be to maintain and strengthen the child's links with their family and community in order to prepare them for this transition. On the other hand, if there is no possibility of rehabilitation home, the aim of the care plan may be for the child to remain in a permanent alternative placement. In this case, the purpose of contact may be to support the child in that placement and/or to help the birth family to give the child permission to attach to new carers.

Sometimes, the aim of the care plan and the purpose of contact will be clear, as when a young person is settled in a long-term placement and the contact arrangements are established. In other cases, the aims of the care plan will change, as when a placement has broken down and the contact arrangements will have to be revised to reflect this.

In practice, you may come across different approaches to care planning. This section looks at contingency, twin track and concurrent care plans. It uses case examples to show how the overall aim of a young person's care plan impacts upon the contact arrangements.

Contingency Planning

In contingency planning, the care plan pursues a fixed aim but also considers what will happen if that aim is not achieved. It is good practice for all care plans to include a contingency plan that can be activated if required.

Twin Tracking

Usually, care plans identify one overall aim. However, in the early stages of a child being looked after, care plans sometimes identify an alternative aim. This is known as 'twin tracking' or 'parallel planning' and is designed to improve permanence planning for looked-after children.

For example, the primary aim of the care plan may be to rehabilitate a child home but *at the same time*, there will be a parallel plan, to move the child to a substitute family if rehabilitation is unsuccessful. In this case, the twin tracks to permanence are: (1) rehabilitation home; and (2) a permanent placement with an alternative family.

Note: with twin tracking/parallel planning there is no expectation that the substitute family will adopt the child if the rehabilitation home is not possible.

Concurrent Planning

In concurrent planning the worker assesses the capacity of the birth parents or wider birth family to parent the child while the child is placed with foster carers. If the assessment concludes that the birth family cannot parent the child, then the young person is adopted by the foster carers. In concurrent planning schemes the foster carers are approved as *both* foster carers *and* adoptive parents.

**Good Practice Checklist:
Assessment and Care Planning**

In summary, assessments in relation to contact should do the following:

✓ comply with legal requirements and statutory guidance;
✓ focus upon the needs of the child;
✓ reflect the aims of the care plan.

Chapter 4 will look at deciding when and where to have contact.

Planning when, where and how

This chapter includes points to consider in relation to when and where to have contact. This will help you to decide about the frequency, timing and length of contact and think about the best venue for both direct and indirect arrangements.

WHEN TO HAVE CONTACT: LEGAL CONSIDERATIONS IN RELATION TO ALL CONTACT ARRANGEMENTS

Promoting 'Reasonable Contact' For Looked-After Children

When considering the length and frequency of the proposed contact arrangements, you should be aware of the 'presumption of reasonable contact' that was discussed in Chapter 1. You also need to comply with your duty to promote contact for looked-after children.

 Point of Law: Promoting Contact

Section 15(1) of the Children Act 1989 says: 'Where a child is being looked after by the local authority, *the authority shall,* unless it is not reasonably practical or consistent with his welfare, *endeavour to promote contact* between the child and (a) his parent, (b) any person who is not a parent of his but has parental responsibility for him, friend or other person connected with him.'

Although the term 'promote' is not defined in legislation, it is generally interpreted to mean that you should actively encourage contact to take place.

 Reminder Box: Giving and Taking Instructions

Remember that if the contact arrangements have been agreed by the court, then you cannot vary these arrangements without the full consultation and agreement of the parties involved, and recourse to the court will be necessary. Legal advisors may tell you that particular types of contact arrangements are more likely to be approved by the courts and it is common for inexperienced workers to feel intimidated by lawyers' understanding of the legal process and their knowledge of current case law. However, the contact arrangements are based upon your assessment of the case, so stick to your guns and ensure that the contact plan remains focused on meeting the needs of the child. Remember that you instruct the lawyer, not the other way around!

Protection from Harmful Contact

While workers have a legal duty to promote reasonable contact, they must also protect children from contact that is harmful. In some circumstances it will be obvious that contact would put people at risk of harm, for example, attempts to abduct a child or assault staff. In such situations workers should take *immediate action* to ensure the safety of the child and their own safety, by securing the building, removing the child to a safe place, and phoning the police.

Often, the risk of harm is more difficult to assess. In practice some children appear upset or are clingy during contact. Some parents may appear to be angry or unco-operative whilst these behaviours are common responses to change and loss, it is understandable that those dealing with this behaviour or its aftermath may see it as harmful. Rather than simply stopping contact, you may consider alternative ways of managing this behaviour, such as by providing additional support or having indirect contact.

Suspending Contact

There may be circumstances where it is advisable to suspend contact temporarily, such as when a child moves placement, it may be preferable to let a child 'settle in' to the placement before arranging contact with previous carers.

In other cases, contact may be suspended at the child's request. Clearly it is unlikely to be in the child's best interest to force the child to maintain contact against their will but it should not be severed permanently until you have spent time with the child looking at the reasons for their refusal. It may be possible to address these and work out alternative ways of maintaining contact.

 Point of Law: Suspending Contact

Section 34(6) of the Children Act 1989 says that if the child is under an Emergency Protection Order, an Interim Care Order or a Care Order, the local authority can suspend contact for up to seven days if it is necessary to safeguard the child or promote the child's welfare.

Section 34(4) of the Children Act 1989 says that after that period of time, contact can *only* be prevented or curtailed by obtaining a court order. So, if contact is suspended, you need to contact your legal services so that court action can be initiated if necessary.

Any proposals to suspend or terminate contact should be considered within the context of the overall aims and objectives of the care plan and should be discussed at the child care review unless circumstances require an urgent decision to be made. If it is not possible to convene a Child Care Review, contact can be suspended for up to seven days without a court order in order to safeguard and promote the child's welfare.

For more detailed information in relation to the suspension or termination of contact for looked-after children, you might like to refer to the Care Planning, Placement and Case Review Regulations 2010 (Department for Education 2010).

Good Practice Point: Keeping the Door Open

Once contact stops, it can be very difficult to re-establish, so rather than ending contact entirely, consider ways of 'keeping the door open'. For example, where direct contact is stopped or suspended, it may still be possible to have indirect contact. Clearly, if there are reasons why the child's whereabouts should not be disclosed, then the exchange of information will have to be done through a third party.

If all contact is stopped, make sure to keep a record of information that the young person can access in the future. Photographs (with names and dates) and letters or cards can be included in a child's life story book. Ensure that copies are kept securely in case the originals are lost or damaged.

Care Planning and Individual Contact Arrangements

As we have seen, the contact arrangements must conform to the legal framework. In order to meet the needs of each child, the contact arrangements should also reflect the overall aims of the care plan.

For example, if the aim of the care plan is to return the child home, the length and frequency of contact will be increased in order to support the plan for reunification. However, when the aim of the care plan is to maintain a young person in an alternative permanent placement, it is likely that the contact will be less frequent. In some cases, the aims of the care plan may mean that the contact between a child and parent is significantly reduced. For example, where the plan is to place a child for adoption, there may be a final direct contact visit and any further contact may be indirect, for example, through letterbox contact or severed completely. For more information about contact arrangements for adopted children, look at the work of Neil and Howe (2010).

Wishes and Feelings of the Child

Section 22(4) of the Children Act 1989 states that the wishes and feelings of the child should be sought in relation to any significant change in their life before a decision is made. While you should ascertain young people's views in relation to contact, you should also explain that not all their requests may be possible.

When setting up the arrangements, think about how significant events may impact upon the timing of contact arrangements, for example, anniversaries, family celebrations. Young people may request to stay overnight with family and friends or go on a school trip. It is important that looked-after children are not made to feel different from their peers and these requests should be facilitated wherever possible. Do ensure that any arrangements for 'extended contact' are made in line with your agency's policies and that you complete any preparation work well in advance.

Reminder Box:
Passport Applications

Obtaining passports for looked-after children can be a source of great frustration to all those involved! Make sure that you allow plenty of time to gather the documentation and get the application and photographs endorsed. Some post offices will check your application before you post it. In order to avoid a last-minute panic make sure that you get this all sorted out *before* the holiday is booked!

As the corporate parent you are responsible for ensuring that contact arrangements meet your legal and the agency's requirements. You also need to make sure that the timing, frequency and length of contact reflect the needs of the young person. Think through both the short-term and long-term implications of the arrangements and ensure there is adequate support to help people cope both physically and emotionally.

When setting up contact arrangements, it may be helpful to consider the following points.

Good Practice Checklist: Points to Bear in Mind

✓ *The age and development of the child*: Arrangements should reflect the needs of the young person. For example, very young children have short-term memories, and regular direct contact may help to maintain relationships, however high frequency contact involving different people and significant travelling time may not benefit that child's development. For older children, an activity-based contact may meet their developmental needs. You may also consider using a combination of direct and indirect contact to meet the needs of a sibling group.

✓ *Routines*: Try and plan contact around established routines. For example, if you are arranging direct contact for small babies, try to minimize disruption to their feeding and sleeping patterns. For older children, arrange contact around school holidays, after-school clubs and other commitments. Contact arrangements should also accommodate the commitments and work patterns of family and carers wherever possible.

✓ *Other contact arrangements*: In some cases, particularly when siblings are placed separately, children may have multiple contact arrangements. Try to keep the plans for contact simple and consider combining contact with other events to prevent 'overload', for example, by arranging contact at a school sports day or encouraging foster carers to arrange visits with siblings in the holidays.

✓ *Visiting procedures*: Some institutions, such as prisons and hospitals, will require you to confirm contact arrangements in advance and/or in writing. Ensure that you check out their procedures and allow sufficient time to comply with these before setting up the visit.

✓ *The logistics of travel*: For children who are placed 'out of area' or want to see family and friends who live a long way from home, think through the logistics of the travel arrangements. Look at a variety of options, such as using public transport or meeting at a venue halfway, to minimize travelling time.

✓ *Special occasions*: If contact is planned to coincide with special occasions, ensure you have a contingency plan in place, for example, if you have arranged for a parent to attend a school play or birthday party, you should phone ahead to check they are en route, or arrange to pick them up yourself or ensure you or a carer can attend if the parents do not turn up.

✓ *Cultural and religious events*: Planning contact around particular events may help a child to maintain their cultural identity, practise their religion and keep links with extended family. When you are planning contact arrangements, think about how these may affect the timing of direct contact visits and have implications for any food or drink consumed during the visit.

WHERE TO HAVE CONTACT

'The right time, right place . . .' Selecting the right venue is important as it 'sets the scene' for both direct and indirect contact arrangements.

Direct Contact

Unless the venue for direct contact is stipulated by the court, it is up to you to decide where to have it. To help select the 'right' locations, take a minute to think about the purpose of contact and what you want to achieve from it. For example, if the purpose of contact is to maintain face-to-face contact between active young siblings, an activity-based contact venue may work well. On the other hand, if the purpose of contact is to build up relationships in preparation for rehabilitation, it can make sense for the visit to be held at the family home.

Indirect Contact

When you are setting up indirect contact, think through the practical issues. Young people in residential care or a foster placement may need access to a phone or a computer. Check that the venue can provide the required privacy as well as the facilities to monitor the indirect contact if necessary.

Clearly, the choice of venue has to be made with the resources you have available but, often, the simplest arrangements work the best.

It may be helpful to think about the following points when deciding where to have contact and, if possible, check out the venue yourself beforehand.

Good Practice Checklist:
The Venue

Facilities

✓ Is the venue clean, tidy and safe?
✓ Is there access to catering facilities, for example, to make hot drinks, warm bottles, prepare snacks?
✓ Are there accessible toilets and baby-changing facilities?
✓ Are there parking spaces on site or nearby?
✓ Are age-appropriate activities available inside and outdoors?
✓ Is the venue open 'out of hours', such as lunchtimes, school holidays?
✓ Is security adequate, for example, staffing, panic buttons, cameras?
✓ Do you need access to a place for religious observance?
✓ Is the building accessible to people with limited mobility?

Layout

✓ Is there enough space for any activities (inside and out)?
✓ Do you need a separate place for people to wait before and after the visit?
✓ Do you want access to a quiet area for discussion?
✓ Does the layout enable discreet and/or 'hands on' supervision?
✓ Is it sufficiently secure?
✓ Do you want a busy or relaxed environment?

Location

✓ Is the venue accessible by public transport?

✓ What is the distance to parents' home and young person's placement?

✓ What is the proximity to local activities, such as the park, playground, café or shops?

✓ Are there areas to avoid, for example, the area around the family home?

Neutrality

✓ Does the venue or area have a negative history?

✓ Is the venue 'neutral' or is it associated with the agency?

Costs and Booking Arrangements

✓ Are the costs approved by your agency, for example, do you need a cost code?

✓ Do you have to book several sessions in advance?

✓ How will the costs of the venue be met, such as by split funding arrangements?

✓ Are there any additional costs, for example, for food, drinks?

Before you make a decision, it might be helpful to think about the advantages and disadvantages of some commonly used venues.

Placements

Contact arrangements should aim to minimize disruption to a child's routine. With adequate planning and support, the young person's placement may provide the ideal venue for occasional or regular contact visits. If the placement is not able to accommodate the whole session, you may consider using it either at the start or the end of a visit.

Around three-quarters of young people who are looked after live in foster placements (BAAF 2011) and although foster parents are not obliged to have contact in their home, the new fostering standards, regulations and guidance make it clear that fostering services should promote the contact arrangements of looked-after children (DCSF 2010). Therefore, it is important to work closely with foster carers and their link workers to consider all possible venues and identify ways in which they can help facilitate the contact arrangements.

Approximately one in ten placements are in residential units; this includes secure units, children's homes and hostels, but occasionally young people are placed in residential schools or other residential settings (BAAF 2011). It is useful to liaise with the residential staff and in particular the young person's key worker to develop creative contact arrangements that facilitate the needs of the child and the family within residential settings.

Reminder Box:
Out of Area Placements

Some young people are placed outside the local authority, and this is known as a placement 'out of area'. This can be for a variety of reasons, such as for their own protection or because of the scarcity of specialist resources in the local authority. Organizing direct contact 'out of area' may have additional implications when you are deciding where to have direct contact, for example, you may have to seek permission to travel outside the local authority or stay overnight.

If it is not feasible to use the placement as a venue for contact, you will have to consider the pros and cons of alternative options.

Good Practice Checklist:
Pros and Cons of Other
Commonly Used Contact Venues

The Family Home

✓ Enables children to see extended family, friends or pets in a familiar environment.

✓ Allows parents and children to share day-to-day activities such as cooking a meal.

✓ Layout may make it difficult to closely monitor or supervise interaction.

✓ Cultural, religious beliefs and celebrations can be observed.

✓ May have negative associations for the young person.

Hostels

✓ May not disclose whereabouts to other agencies.

✓ Access may be restricted to certain groups, for example, women's hostels may not admit males.

✓ Often a secure venue.

Family Centres

✓ Centre staff may be available to supervise, support or record contact visit.

✓ Designed to be child-friendly.

✓ Often experienced in facilitating contact arrangements.

Prison/Young Offenders Institution

✓ Visiting may be restricted.

✓ Can be an intimidating environment, for example, security checks, restrictions on physical contact.
✓ Advanced checks and ID may be required.

Hospitals and Hospices

✓ Visiting may be restricted.
✓ Can be an unfamiliar environment, for example, medical equipment, patients' physical appearance.
✓ Specialist liaison staff may be available to support the visit.

School

✓ Contact may be incorporated into school activity so parents can recognize their child's achievements, for example, sports day.
✓ Provides opportunity to build relationships informally, as parents meet teaching staff.

Social Work Office

✓ Formal environment.
✓ Generally not equipped to facilitate contact.
✓ Experienced staff available to support.
✓ May be preferable to cancelling the visit.

Non-Traditional Venues

Contact can be enjoyable! So think about using venues that enable young people to pursue their interests and to have fun. Airport viewing stations, motorbike rallies, going fishing, playing games or having a picnic in the park can all work well.

Example from Practice: Think about the Association of the Venue

As the duty worker, Neil was asked to arrange a direct contact visit between Maisy and her 3-year-old daughter, Charlotte, who was subject to an interim care order. The contact arrangements had to be made quickly and, to save time, Neil texted the details of the visit to Maisy. When Neil and Charlotte arrived for the contact visit, Maisy was waiting outside. She was very upset and told Neil that she did not want to go into the building because she had recently been there for a final contact meeting with her oldest child who had been adopted.

Venue to Conform with the Requirements of the Agency

While statutory responsibilities are outlined in primary and secondary legislation, your role and responsibilities in relation to contact are also determined by the policies and procedures of your agency. Ensure you are familiar with those that relate specifically to contact, such as guidance on core contact hours, as well as generic policies, such as about lone working or expenses, which may also impact upon contact arrangements.

Good Practice Checklist: Check Your Agency's Policies

Before setting up contact arrangements, you should ensure you understand your agency's policies in relation to the following.

Criteria Used

✓ What criteria are used to prioritize work, for example, how are cases in proceedings prioritized?

✓ Are arrangements based on 'core contact hours', that is, the minimum and maximum levels of contact for particular groups of looked-after children?

✓ How are resources managed? Are there guidelines about financial support towards travel, food and activities?

✓ What are the criteria for reducing, suspending and stopping contact arrangements?

The Roles and Responsibilities of Those Involved

✓ Are contact arrangements 'contracted out', for example, to a voluntary agency or an in-house contact team?

✓ What are the contracted responsibilities of all those involved? Are foster carers required to facilitate contact?

✓ Who is responsible for 'signing off' or endorsing contact arrangements?

✓ How are complaints managed?

Methods of Communication

✓ How do you make referrals to other agencies involved in managing contact?

✓ What are the procedures for communicating changes to the contact arrangements, for example, changes of worker, new information that impacts upon the risk assessment?

✓ How do you contact the agency in emergency or out of hours, for example, if the car breaks down, or a child absconds?

✓ What are the procedures about recording, sharing and reviewing information about contact?

Good Practice Point:
If You Don't Know, Ask

If you need specific guidance or clarification about your statutory obligations or do not understand your agency's policies in relation to a particular case, it is advisable to speak with your line manager and/or legal services *before* you set up the contact arrangements.

As you gain experience of setting up contact arrangements you will begin to recognize that certain arrangements 'fit' with particular circumstances.

- Supported direct contact at a neutral venue may work well when there is a history of animosity between family members.
- Direct unsupervised contact at home may be suitable if the assessment indicates that the needs of the child can be met by the family during contact visits.
- Infrequent indirect contact may be used to maintain relationships when face-to-face contact no longer meets the child's needs or direct contact is not possible.
- Supervised direct contact in an agency venue may suit situations when the child needs to be safeguarded but wants reassurance that the parent is physically OK.

Good Practice Checklist: Decisions Made

Now you have gathered and 'weighed up' the evidence, you will be able to make a decision on the following elements:

✓ the type of contact that will best meet the child's needs – direct or indirect or combination of both;
✓ supervision and monitoring requirements – level and purpose;
✓ the frequency of contact;
✓ who is involved in the contact arrangements – roles and tasks;
✓ suitable contact venues;
✓ what supports are required before, during and after contact;
✓ how to manage risk and ensure adequate safeguards;
✓ complying with statutory and agency requirements;
✓ the resources and time you have available.

5 Drawing up the contact agreement

This chapter looks at drawing up direct and indirect contact agreements for young people who are looked after. There are many points to consider in negotiating the terms of the contact agreement, for both direct and indirect contact, and making it work for all the parties concerned. An example of a contact agreement is given in this chapter as a template for you to use.

NEGOTIATING THE TERMS

Working in Partnership

When a young person becomes 'looked after', the parents relinquish their parental responsibility and the local authority becomes the corporate parent. Good practice guidelines promote the idea of working 'in partnership' with parents, but bear in mind that parents have not usually entered into this partnership willingly. When you are planning contact arrangements, try to negotiate an 'agreement' rather than impose a 'plan'. Involving families throughout the process means they are more likely to buy into the contact agreement and stick to it. If family members are unwilling to meet face to face, you could consider using an independent broker such as a friend or a family mediation service to help negotiate the agreement.

**Reminder Box:
Young People Who Are
Accommodated**

If a child is accommodated under Section 20 of the Children Act 1989, the parents still have parental responsibility for their child. This means that they must be consulted about contact arrangements and their wishes should be adhered to *unless* there is evidence that this would be detrimental to the child's welfare. In this case, the local authority may consider making an application to the court for a care order.

Incorporate Support

Contact can be a difficult and emotional time for children, families, carers and staff. So when you are making plans for contact, think about the practical and emotional supports that can be built in to help people cope.

In supervised direct contact, it may be helpful for the supervisor to provide 'hands on' support, for example, by introducing games or help to manage challenging behaviour. Where direct contact is unsupervised, you could support the arrangements by helping with transport or the cost of activities. With indirect contact arrangements, the child and/or the parents may need support to write letters, choose presents or make phone calls.

Remember that the need for support may be more acute *after* contact. Make sure to check in with the child, the parents and the carers regularly to review the arrangements and the supports in place.

The terms of each contact agreement will be different but the following checklists include some of the points you may consider when planning all contact arrangements, as well as specific considerations in relation to direct and indirect contact.

Good Practice Checklist: Points to Consider When Planning Contact

Comply with Statutory and Agency Requirements

✓ Ensure the arrangements comply with any directions from the court.

✓ Check that the purpose of contact reflects the overall aim of the young person's care plan.

✓ Make sure that the proposed arrangement conform to the policies of your agency, such as insurance procedures.

Ensure the Type and Purpose of Contact Are Explicit

✓ Clarify the type of contact involved, for example, direct, indirect or a combination of both.

✓ Discuss the arrangements with all those involved to ensure that they all understand the purpose of the contact.

✓ If contact arrangements include any formal assessments, for example, an assessment of parenting capacity, this needs to be made explicit.

Take into Account the Needs of those Involved

✓ Make sure the arrangements take into account the young person's age and understanding.

✓ Take into account any additional need that may impact upon the arrangements, such as medical conditions that may affect mobility.

✓ Think about whether people will cope with the arrangements. It may be better to organize contact for small children in the morning when they are less tired.

Consider the Timing of the Contact

✓ Think about how the arrangements fit with the participants' other commitments, such as after-school activities, work patterns, holiday plans.

✓ Be aware of other significant contact arrangements, for example, those relating to siblings or other children in placement.

✓ If the contact has an assessment function, think about how the structure and timeframe of the assessment process will impact upon the contact arrangements.

✓ Decide upon the start date of the contact arrangements.

✓ Bear in mind that special occasions, such as birthdays or religious festivals may be compromised if people, cards or presents fail to arrive, so consider arranging alternatives to these significant times.

Identify Those Involved

✓ Clearly identify those who are involved in the contact arrangements, having the full names and contact details of all family members and the professionals involved.

✓ Have details of people who *may not* have contact, as you may need to circulate descriptions or photographs to carers or security staff.

Safeguard Arrangements

✓ Update the risk assessments to quantify the current risks and to ensure that safeguards relate to specific risks.

✓ Consider the need for separate contact plans if there are multiple contact arrangements, for example, if there is animosity between parents or if siblings have separate contact without parents.

Agree Expectations and Ground Rules

✓ Clarify roles and responsibilities in relation to contact, for example, that the social worker takes responsibility for arranging the venue or that the carer helps the child write a letter to a parent.

✓ Agree the ground rules at the start and explain the consequences of unacceptable behaviour.

Build in Adequate Support

✓ Clarify the arrangements for providing emotional support to the child and family before, during and after the contact visit. For example, the social worker may phone the young person after contact, or a parent may attend a support group.

✓ Consider whether additional support is required at specific times, such as at the beginning or end of the contact visits, or during times of additional stress such as anniversaries.

✓ Think about how the contact arrangements impact on you and identify the support you may need.

Plan for Contingencies

✓ Identify any likely difficulties, such people failing to make contact, and have a 'Plan B' to fall back on.
✓ Agree the best way of notifying the participants of last-minute changes to the contact agreements, such as by text message.

Record Contact

✓ Clarify the purpose of record keeping. Think about what will be recorded and by whom.
✓ Identify the procedures and formats that are used by your agency to record contact.
✓ Decide how the contact records will be communicated and who may access them.

Evaluate and Review the Arrangements

✓ Ensure people understand the criteria that will be used to evaluate the contact arrangements, for example, how the desired outcomes will be measured and recorded.
✓ Identify the process of approving, reviewing and changing the contact agreement.
✓ Agree a date to review the arrangements.

There may be particular points to consider when planning direct contact arrangements.

Good Practice Checklist: Direct Contact Arrangements

Clarify the Supervision Arrangements

✓ Ensure that the role of the supervisor is clear. Are they there simply to observe or do they have a more 'hands-on' role?

✓ Ensure that the purpose and level of supervision are clear to the supervisor and that they have clear instructions, such as whether to intervene if the parent attempts to give child information through non-verbal signs.

Managing Risks

✓ Identify specific risks and the safeguards that are in place to manage them. If there is a risk of physical harm, think about whether parents should accompany the young person to the toilet or prepare food for them.

✓ Consider whether the use of recording equipment such as cameras and phones is permissible during contact.

Thinking through the Practicalities

✓ Specify the areas and venues that can be used and those that cannot, for example, state whether outings into the community are allowed as part of the contact visit.

✓ If there is a history of family conflict, decide where people may congregate before and after the visit.

✓ Clarify how expenses will be met, such as the cost of refreshments and travel.

✓ Agree the transport arrangements, for example, whether carers transport the child, or whether parents make their own way.

✓ Think about the resources you will need, such as wheelchairs, prams, car seats, insurance cover.
✓ Clarify the mechanism for updating and circulating contact information.

Contingency Planning

✓ Consider introducing checks prior to planned contact. If parents have a history of non-attendance, you could arrange to phone them just before the visit to ensure they are on their way.
✓ Make sure that you think about alternative activities and venues in case of last-minute changes.

There may be particular points to consider when planning indirect contact arrangements.

Good Practice Checklist: Indirect Contact Arrangements

Reviewing the Purpose of Indirect Contact

✓ Specify the reason for indirect (rather than direct) contact.
✓ Ensure that the decision to have indirect contact is based on an accurate and recent assessment.
✓ Consider the possibility of combining indirect and direct contact.

Methods of Indirect Contact

✓ Think about which method of indirect contact reflects the young person's age and development (such as Skype, DVD, email, letter, social networking).

✓ If the young person's whereabouts should not be disclosed, consider ways of editing information that would enable a child to be identified (such as logos on school photographs, addresses on letters and emails).

✓ Take into account procedures of other agencies. For example, prisons may restrict types of communication such as emails, DVDs.

Coordinating the Exchange of Information

✓ Clarify the arrangements, for example, does the parent write to child first?

How frequently is information exchanged?

✓ Specify where the communication should be sent. To the social worker's office or the foster carers' home?

✓ If letterbox contact is used, ensure you have the details of the agencies involved in the letterbox contact. Is it operated 'in-house' or through an independent agency?

✓ If the letterbox is currently 'non-operational', make sure you know how it is activated.

✓ Check that you understand how indirect operates, such as where correspondence is sent to. Is it opened and 'vetted' before it is passed on? Does it require a 'unique identifier'?

✓ Confirm that the contact details of the participants are accurate, for example, if the parents have moved house or child has moved placement.

Support

✓ Identify the practical support people require to maintain indirect contact, for example, the young person's social worker may assist parents to write letters or to select a gift for their child.

✓ Think about how people will be supported emotionally, for example, if they receive no communication or receive upsetting news.

Establishing Ground Rules

✓ Is there agreement about what people are called? For example, the birth Mum may sign letters 'Mummy Carol'.
✓ Try and reach agreement about budgets and the practicalities of exchanging gifts. The use of gift vouchers may ensure presents are age-appropriate and delivered easily.

Safeguarding

✓ Is the content of the communication monitored before it is sent on?
✓ What type of information is deemed 'unsuitable' to be passed on and how will this be removed?
✓ How is information 'vetted'? By the social worker opening letters, the foster carers listening to phone calls, accessing emails?
✓ Check that any monitoring arrangements are clear to the participants.

LACK OF CONTINGENCY PLANNING

In practice, contact plans can be derailed for all sorts of reasons. The young person or parents may fall ill, other people may attend without prior agreement. There may be problems with transport or the contact venue may be unavailable at the last minute. When you are planning contact arrangements, ensure you have a 'Plan B' to cover such situations and ensure you have up-to-date details of the people involved and their mobile numbers, so you can communicate the contingency plan at short notice.

Sometimes, contingency planning can be built into the contact arrangements, as this example from practice shows.

Example from Practice: Contingency Planning

David, aged 10, has lived with his foster carers for two years. It is a permanent placement and it is unlikely that he will return home. David has unsupervised direct contact with Margaret, his Mum. They meet each month for tea at Mum's house. Margaret has enduring health problems which require regular admissions to hospital. A couple of hours before the contact visit, the foster carers phone Margaret to check she is OK to see David. If she is too unwell to attend, another date is then arranged.

WRITING THE CONTACT AGREEMENT

Once you have negotiated the terms of the contact arrangements, it is time to write the contact agreement. In practice, it is unlikely that any contact agreement will satisfy all of the people all of the time. Your role is to balance the views of all the participants and negotiate an agreement that satisfies most of the people most of the time while keeping the needs of the child at the centre.

In some cases, for example, where assessments are ongoing, it may not be clear what the final contact arrangements will be. This does not mean that you should prevaricate and do nothing. Agree an interim plan. It is better to have a temporary agreement than none at all!

Contact agreements should be short and focus specifically on the arrangements for that child. They should not be seen as an opportunity to demonstrate literary talent! Their purpose is simply to explain:

- what will be done;
- how it will be done;

■ when it will be done;
■ who will do it.

Example from Practice:
A Direct Contact Agreement

This is an example of a direct contact agreement that was written by Alice Smith, the social worker for Charlie Shaw (aged 7). Two years ago the court granted a care order as a result of physical harm to Charlie by his step-father, Chris. Chris still lives with Charlie's Mum, Laura Collins. There is no plan to rehabilitate Charlie home and he is placed with long-term foster carers. Charlie has a medical condition which means he is often ill. Laura has a mild learning difficulty. She has a history of missing contact visits and sometimes she arrives with Chris. Charlie likes to see his Mum. He does not want any contact with Chris and becomes angry and throws things around if Laura talks about Chris during the visit.

Contact agreement for Charlie Shaw

*This is the contact agreement between Charlie Shaw and Laura Collins.
This agreement starts on the 1st Jan 20 . . . .*
*Charlie and Laura will meet every four weeks at the Midtown
Family Centre.*
*During term time, contact visits will be from 3.30 to 5pm on Tuesday
afternoons. In the school holidays, contact visits will be from 1 to
2.30pm on Tuesday afternoons.*
*Transport for Charlie will be arranged by the local authority. Laura will
arrange her own transport.*
This agreement will be reviewed on 1st June 20 . . .
We agree the following:
*Laura will telephone the family centre half an hour before every contact
visit to confirm she is able to attend.*
*A social worker or a member of the contact team will stay with Charlie and
support the visit by helping Laura to play and engage with Charlie. They will
intervene to help Laura to manage Charlie's behaviour if necessary.*
*The people named in this agreement may attend the contact. Anyone who
attends the visit without prior agreement with the social worker will be
asked to leave.*

If Charlie is unwell and/or the contact session needs to be cancelled by the local authority, a member of the Social Work Team will telephone Laura before the visit. Another visit will be arranged if possible.
Laura will telephone the social worker on 012345 or the family centre on 67891 if she is unable to attend the contact visit.
If Laura misses three consecutive visits and does not provide an adequate reason for not attending contact with Charlie, a meeting will be arranged with the social worker to review this contact agreement.

... ... Laura Collins (Mother)
... ... Alice Smith (Social Worker)
... ... Cheryl Sanders (Social Work Team Manager)
... ... Bob Wright (Manager of Midtown Family Centre)

The contact details, map and directions for finding the Social Work Team and the Midtown Family Centre are on the back of this agreement.
If any of your contact details change, please let Alice Smith know as soon as possible.

Good Practice Checklist: Communicating the Arrangements

Do not assume that information shared is information understood! In some cases you will have been involved in setting up the contact arrangements from the start. In other cases, the contact arrangements have been agreed. The following checklist may help to ensure that the plan has been communicated effectively.

✓ Check the date of the contact agreement and ensure that everyone is working to the current version.
✓ Ensure the arrangements have been circulated to all the agencies involved.

✓ Make sure that the arrangements are communicated clearly.
   They may need to be translated or presented in large print. If
   people have learning difficulties, think about using diaries or
   pictures.

✓ Review the arrangements with those involved before contact
   is due to take place to ensure you are all 'on the same page'.

✓ Make sure that the contact agreement is written down and
   filed in the right place – not left in your drawer – so it is
   easily accessible to colleagues who may need to see it.

Example from Practice: Failing to Communicate the Arrangements

As a newly qualified social worker, Sarah took over a number of cases
from Ted, an experienced worker who was retiring. At the handover
meeting, Ted told Sarah about the well-established contact arrangements
that were in place for a large group of traveller children and Maggie,
their Mum. Keen to make a good impression, Sarah noted the details,
added the dates of the next contact visits and posted a copy of the
contact arrangements to Maggie. When she did not show up for the
following contact visit, Sarah called at Maggie's house. When she asked
about the contact visit, Maggie said that Ted had not called to tell her
about it. Sarah explained that she had sent the details in a letter. 'Sure,
what is the point of that?' Maggie said, 'I don't read.'

**Good Practice Checklist:
Drafting the Contact Agreement**

Once you have drafted the agreement, ask yourself:

✓ Are the arrangements clear?
✓ Do they fulfil your legal obligations?
✓ Do they conform to agency policy?
✓ Do they reflect what people want and can cope with?
✓ Are there sufficient resources to support the arrangements?
✓ Would these arrangements be good enough for your child?

Now we have drafted the agreement, the next step is to put it into action. The final three chapters go on to look at how to manage, evaluate and record contact.

6 Managing contact

This chapter goes on to look at putting contact agreements into action. It includes points to consider before, during and after contact takes place and includes case examples to suggest ways of managing direct and indirect contact arrangements.

Reminder Box: Your Role in the Process

Remember that the way you manage contact depends on your role. For example, if you are the allocated worker for a looked-after child and there are no contact arrangements in place, you will need to make an assessment of the information in order to develop a plan. On the other hand, if you are facilitating an existing contact arrangement on behalf of the allocated worker, your role is to implement the plan that is already in place.

As we have seen, it is important that contact arrangements comply with statutory requirements and the policies and procedures of your agency. Remember that the purpose of contact is to benefit the child so don't forget to think about the quality as well as the quantity of the arrangements.

Example from Practice: Focus on Quality Not Quantity

A looked-after children team I worked in undertook a review of contact arrangements and asked those involved what made for 'good' contact (Key and Scott 2007). Responses included:

"A chance to show our family that we love and care for them and receive it back.
(young person)

When the rights of the children and parents are respected equally.
(parent)

Good prior planning and communication between all the parties and agencies involved.
(social worker)

Based on a formal contract agreed with the family.
(contact worker)

A good relationship between the parent and the worker helps."
(foster carer)

Keeping the focus on the quality of contact encourages you to adopt a creative and collaborative approach to managing the arrangements which should make it easier for the child, the family and you!

DIRECT CONTACT

Whatever your role, it is important to review the arrangements before you start. The following checklist may help you to avoid some of the common pitfalls workers encounter when managing direct and indirect contact in practice.

Common Pitfalls: Avoiding Common Pitfalls in Direct Contact

Review the Contact Arrangements

✓ Make sure you understand the purpose and detail of the contact arrangements.

✓ Are people's tasks and responsibilities clear?

✓ What level of supervision is required?

✓ Check details of who is and who is not allowed to attend contact.

✓ Identify the known risks and safeguards that are in place.

✓ Review the last contact records and check for changes to previous arrangements.

Think Through the Practicalities

✓ Has the most recent plan been communicated to those involved?

✓ How will you identify people you have not met previously?

✓ Check that you have complied with requirements for all agencies involved, for example, a prison will require advanced notification, schools or hospitals will require identification.

✓ Prepare people in advance about any big changes in their family's circumstances, such as new partners or siblings, illnesses or deaths.

✓ Have you got the phone numbers and addresses, including mobile numbers and post codes, of all those involved in the contact?

✓ Do you need directions or a navigation aid?

✓ Have you allowed enough time for the journey. Check for delays or cancellations.

✓ Check that vehicle, including pool cars, are adequately equipped. Do you have car seats, childproof locks, seat belts?

✓ Ensure travel arrangements comply with your agency's procedures, regarding the use of your own vehicle, insurance cover, restrictions on mileage and expenses.

✓ Have you got enough supplies for the journey and during the visit, such as toys, games, drinks or snacks?

✓ Are you prepared for young children – bottles, nappies, baby wipes, spare clothes?

✓ Have you got details of any allergies/medication children need during visit?

✓ Check you have a mobile phone that is charged, with coverage and charger.

✓ Can you meet the costs of contact? Do you need cash, credit card for petrol, details of cost code?

Contingency Planning

✓ Have you communicated your plan? Does your agency know about the contact arrangements and when to raise the alert if you are not back?

✓ Does your manager know your mobile phone number, car registration number, home address?

✓ Do your plans comply with your agency's 'buddy' system or lone worker policy?

✓ Do you know who to contact in an emergency?

✓ What is the 'Plan B', if people are late or do not show up?

Good Practice Point: Going Equipped

It is a good idea to have box in the office or in the back of your car full of different things that can be used at indoor and outdoor contact visits, such as footballs, puzzles, colouring books, toys, DVDs.

Checklist: Arriving at Direct Contact

✓ Make sure that people know each other and understand their roles and responsibilities in relation to supervisors or interpreters.

✓ Check that the facilities and layout are safe. Check fire exits and toilets.

✓ If necessary, remind people of the purpose of contact. If contact is part of assessment, check that people understand this.

✓ If necessary, explain the supervision/support/recording arrangements.

✓ Confirm the time the visit will end and the arrangements at the end of contact.

✓ Make sure your car is parked nearby so that you can get out easily if necessary.

In practice, people will not always stick to the letter of contact agreements. They may be a couple of minutes late or forget to attend a visit. In practice, you can address most minor lapses informally by reminding people of their commitment to the agreement. If the pattern persists, a more formal 'agreement meeting' chaired by a manager may be necessary.

Example from Practice: Managing Unexpected Arrivals

Eve is a single Mum. Her twin sons Eli and Sam (aged 6) were removed from her care as a result of chronic neglect and non-accidental injury. The contact visits are at a family centre and are supervised by Louise, the children's social worker. Eve is often late for contact visits but today she arrives early with her new partner. Eve tells Louise that she and her new partner are getting married and that he wants to see the boys and be assessed to care for them. Louise takes Eve and her partner into a side room. She acknowledges their wishes but explains that alterations to the contact arrangements have to be discussed in advance, that the boys do not know Eve's new partner and that he will not be able to attend today's visit. Eve is not happy about this but Louise reminds her of the terms of the contact plan and says, 'This is not the arrangement we had agreed for today.' She arranges to meet with Eve and her partner the following week to discuss their request.

During the Visit

Your role during contact will depend upon the purpose of the visit and the level of supervision that is required. For example, if the purpose of contact is to promote parent–child interaction, you may intervene to support the parent to play with the child or to help manage challenging behaviour. It may also be necessary to be physically close to those involved in order to provide close supervision, in response to concerns about physical harm. Be mindful that your 'support' may be viewed differently by those receiving it.

If contact is being used to assess behaviour, such as the interaction between parent and child, think about the 'light in the fridge phenomenon'. When making your assessment, bear in mind that people behave differently when they are being observed and remember that you only see what is happening when the fridge light is on.

Direct contact visits can be an emotional and anxious time for all those involved and conflict can manifest itself in a number of ways during the contact visit. Sibling rivalry may result in children arguing, fighting or vying for parents' attention. Young people's conflicting allegiances to birth and foster families can also make children prone to exaggerate and/or tell lies, appear ambivalent and, or clingy.

For many parents, direct contact is very difficult and this might create conflict in other ways. For example, parents' resistance to a child's care plan may be demonstrated by departing from the terms of the contact arrangements or attempting to undermine the placement. As you gain experience of managing direct contact with families, you will become more attuned to 'gauging the temperature' and anticipating the potential 'flashpoints'.

Good Practice Point: 'Accentuate the Positive'

Try to enjoy contact! As you become more confident, you will develop your own style but adopting a positive attitude will make it easier to 'eliminate the negative'. Some practitioner's tips about accentuating the positive include:

- Be realistic and fair in your expectations and tolerances.
- Handle power imbalances in a firm and sensitive way.
- Maintain a sense of humour!

Goodbye or Final Contacts

Goodbye or final contacts are arranged when the overall aim of the care plan is to sever contact between a child and their parents, such as in cases where the aim of the care plan is to place a child for adoption.

In practice, final contact visits can be emotionally charged occasions for everyone involved and will need careful and considerate planning. Make sure that the child, the family and the carers are prepared for the visit and have adequate support during and afterwards. It is unlikely that the parents will seek support from you at this time so try to ensure they are supported by a family member or an independent professional.

It is also advisable to revisit the risk assessment prior to the visit. This may be the last time a parent sees their child and this may increase the likelihood of particular risks, such as abduction or harm to staff. In the light of the assessment you may consider introducing additional safeguards such as using a secure venue or increasing the level of supervision.

Ending the Contact Visit

Ensure that you have thought about how to manage the end of the visit. You may need parents to leave before the children, or may want extra support from other staff to facilitate transport. People may need help to end the visit, so as the finishing time approaches, consider reminding people that the visit is ending soon and at the end of the session help people say goodbyes if necessary.

Checklist: After Contact

✓ The child and/or their family may need support after the visit to 'process' how it went and think about the impact it may have on future sessions. This may be given through a visit or follow-up phone call.

✓ Carers often have to deal with the 'fall-out' after contact visits. Try and liaise with their link worker to ensure they have the support they need.

✓ After each contact visit, you should informally review what worked well and identify any concerns that need to be addressed before the next visit.

✓ If the visit was supervised by someone else, ensure you get feedback from them.

✓ Ensure that the file record of contact is updated, for example, change of address, telephone number.

✓ Update colleagues of any new information that will affect future contact arrangements, such as the level of supervision required.

✓ Seek reimbursement for expenses incurred.

✓ Ensure that the arrangements for next contact are clear.

INDIRECT CONTACT

In some cases, 'face-to-face' contact will be supplemented by indirect contact. For example, if a child is placed a long way from family and friends, they may see each other every couple of months and have telephone contact in between. In other cases, all contact may be indirect, if there is a risk of the child being harmed or being given inappropriate information.

The following section includes points to consider in relation to indirect contact.

Good Practice Checklist: Indirect Contact

Before Indirect Contact

✓ Decide on the most appropriate means of communication, such as letter, Skype, email, text.

✓ Think about the support people may need to manage indirect contact, for example to write/read a letter, access a computer.

✓ Consider how the content of the information can be monitored. Will someone open presents and read all letters before they are passed on to the child?

✓ Think about ways of recording and tracking indirect contact. It will not always be practical to document texts and mobile telephone calls.

✓ Be realistic about managing the exchange of information. Nowadays many young people will have access to mobile phones and the internet and will know their home address.

✓ Think about what people will be called, for example, the child may use 'Mummy' to refer to birth mother or the foster carer.

✓ Will contact be one-way – where the child contacts the parent – or two-way – where child and parent contact each other?

✓ Clarify who will make the first contact.

✓ Think about the frequency and timing of indirect contact, whether this should coincide with birthdays or religious celebration and the implications of contact not occurring at these significant times.

✓ Consider whether indirect contact should include the exchange of gifts or tokens. Think about the practicalities of exchanging these.

✓ Think about the long term. For example, if there is currently no contact, a 'non-operational' letterbox contact can be set up and activated later.

During Contact

✓ Think about who can facilitate and monitor indirect contact. For example, the foster carer may assist the child to make phone calls or a contact service may co-ordinate the exchange of materials, such as letters, photographs, via a third party.

✓ What happens if either one or both parties do not maintain contact?

After Contact

✓ Check whether indirect contact happened as planned.

✓ The child and/or their family may need support after indirect contact or when indirect contact does not happen as planned, such as when birthday cards containing inappropriate information are not passed to the child.

✓ Carers often have to deal with the 'fall-out' when indirect contact is not made. Check that they have the support they need to support the child.

✓ Ensure that the file record of contact is updated for change of address or telephone number.

✓ Continue to review the arrangements to ensure this is the best way of maintaining contact.

7 Evaluating the contact

This chapter looks at ways of evaluating and reviewing the contact arrangements. Most practitioners will tell you that their errors and mistakes have been a source of great learning. However, ongoing evaluation is a less dramatic and equally useful means of identifying what works well and what needs to change. This chapter shows how the process of evaluation will help you to reflect on your practice in order to plan future contact arrangements.

THE BENEFITS OF EVALUATION

Evaluating the contact arrangements allows you to stand back and view the bigger picture. This helps you to do the following:

- Clarify roles and responsibilities.
- Inform decisions and resolve uncertainty.
- Integrate theoretical learning into your practice.
- Re-evaluate your personal beliefs and emotional responses.
- Identify emerging trends and/or dangerous practice.
- Find solutions to practical and emotional barriers.
- Share good practice.

Methods of Evaluation

In practice, contact arrangements are evaluated in both planned and unplanned ways. Planned evaluations include:

- supervision with your line manager
- statutory review
- multi-agency meeting
- transfer of case to another worker or team
- announced inspections or audits.

Unplanned evaluations can occur as a result of the following:

- a change in the child's circumstances, such as placement breakdown;
- complaints or allegation of malpractice;
- formal feedback from child or family;
- an investigation as part of a Serious Case Review.

**Good Practice Point:
Reflective Practice**

Adopting a reflective approach encourages you to evaluate your practice as you go along. The process of critical reflection will help you to clarify the reasons for your decisions, identify the strengths and weaknesses of the current plan and anticipate questions that you may be asked in any planned and unplanned evaluations of the contact arrangements.

Donald Schön considers how workers become more reflective practitioners. He makes the distinction between 'reflection in action' and 'reflection on action' (Schön 1983). Put simply, reflection 'in action' occurs when you evaluate what you are doing *as you are doing it* in order to do something about it immediately. Reflection 'on action' occurs when you evaluate what you have done *after the event* in order to inform future practice.

In practice, you reflect 'in' and 'on' action every day. This process of evaluation helps you to critically reflect upon and learn from your practice and develop confidence in your professional judgement.

Workers' professional confidence and judgement can be nurtured by the development of a 'learning culture' within their organization.

Professor Munro's review of child protection practice in 2011 suggests that

> A move from a compliance to a learning culture will require those working in child protection to be given more scope to exercise professional judgment in deciding how best to help children and their families. It will require more determined and robust management at the front line to support the development of professional confidence.
>
> (Department for Education 2011: 5)

You may find the following points can help you to reflect upon your practice and also promote a learning culture within your organization.

Evaluate as You Go Along

- Ask yourself 'What if?' questions, for example, 'What would happen if the visit was elsewhere?'
- Do a quick 'SWOT analysis' to identify the strengths, weaknesses, opportunities and threats of the current contact arrangements.

Example from Practice: Reflection 'In Action'

At a contact visit during the school holidays, Emily met her two boys (aged 4 and 5) in the family centre for a supervised contact visit. After a few minutes the children started to argue and vie for Emily's attention. The contact worker suggested that the boys play a ball game outside with their Mum and asked Emily to explain the rules before they begin. This structured activity enabled Emily to 'referee' the game and share attention between her sons.

Get Feedback

Ask the child, their family or colleagues for their views about the current arrangements. You may even consider being filmed or observed as you facilitate contact to see yourself from other people's perspective.

> ### Example from Practice: Reflection 'On Action'
>
> Chris found that managing bi-annual direct contact for three children who maintained contact with two adopted siblings was time-consuming and hard to supervise. Following advice from a colleague, Chris got in touch with the social worker from the adoption team and they agreed in future to share tasks such as arranging venues and transporting children.

Incorporate Evaluation into Recording

When you are updating contact records or reviewing contact plans, use 'What? Where? When? and How?' questions to prompt and structure your thinking.

Think about the Impact of Self

Be honest about your own fears and aspirations in relation to the contact arrangements. Ask yourself questions such as, 'What did I want to see happen?', 'How would I feel if this did not happen?'

The following case example shows how supervision can be used to evaluate contact arrangements in order to inform future planning.

> ### Example from Practice: Evaluating Contact Arrangements in Supervision
>
> Andy is a social worker responsible for managing direct contact visits for two sisters, aged 10 and 12, who are placed together with newly qualified foster carers. The girls have weekly unsupervised contact

with Jill, their Mum, at the foster carer's house. Yesterday Andy received a phone call from the girls' foster carer. She tells him that Jill has been late for the last three contacts and at the last visit she had arrived at the house 'spaced out'. The foster carer acknowledges that she did not know much about drugs but she was concerned about having future contact visits at the house. Andy talked with the girls who provided a similar account of Jill's behaviour saying they didn't like to see their Mum in that state. When Andy addressed these concerns with Jill she became upset and said she was late because the bus timetable had changed. She admitted smoking a joint before the last visit but this was the only time this had occurred and that it would not happen again. The girls' care plan is due to be reviewed in two weeks and before the statutory review Andy arranges supervision with his line manager to evaluate the contact arrangements.

PREPARING TO EVALUATE CONTACT

When you are evaluating contact arrangements it can be helpful to look at things from the perspective of the child and family, the agency as well as your own! You may consider the following questions.

From the Child's and Family's Perspective

Do the contact arrangements:

■ 'fit' with the overall aim of the care plan?
■ reflect the age and interests of the child?
■ have appropriate levels of supervision?
■ take the child's view into account?

From the Agency's Perspective

Do the contact arrangements:

■ fulfil statutory requirements?
■ comply with policy and procedures?

■ use resources effectively?
■ clarify roles and responsibilities?

From the Worker's Perspective

Do the contact arrangements:

■ work within the time and resources available?
■ apportion tasks fairly?
■ include adequate support and safeguards?

Example from Practice: Evaluating Contact Arrangements in Supervision, Further Steps

In supervision, Andy identified that the overall aim of the girl's care plan is to return the girls to Jill's care and that direct contact is being gradually built up to prepare for their rehabilitation home. He confirmed that previously, unsupervised contact had gone well and there were no other concerns in relation to Mum's behaviour.

Analysing the evidence helped Andy to weigh up the likelihood and severity of the risks inherent in the current arrangements. For example, he felt that it was unlikely that a re-occurrence of Mum's behaviour would place the girls at immediate risk of significant harm.

However, Andy's line manager noted that the carer's concerns about unsupervised direct contact at their home might eventually jeopardize the security of the placement which might expose the girls to other, more significant risks.

Andy and his supervisor agreed that temporary additional safeguards should be introduced to support the foster carers to continue to facilitate the direct contact. The following actions were agreed:

■ Jill to phone or text Andy an hour before the contact visit to confirm she would be attending on time.
■ Andy to meet Mum at a café near the foster carer's house 10 minutes before the contact visit to ensure she does not attend contact under the influence of drugs.
■ Andy to check alternative public transport links.

- Andy to liaise with Jill, the foster carers and their link worker prior to next contact visit to re-arrange time of contact and agree the implementation of additional safeguards.
- Andy to amend the contact plan to reflect changes and circulate to those involved.
- Andy to inform I R O of reason for changes to contact arrangements prior to the statutory review.
- Link worker to review need to provide additional training with foster carers about substance misuse.
- Andy and his manager to meet with Jill in one month to review the supervision arrangements.

SUMMARY

The evaluation stage enables you to reflect on your practice, transform experience into knowledge and understanding in order to inform future contact arrangements. So, when you are evaluating contact arrangements, try to do the following:

- Evaluate informally and make changes as you go along.
- Keep the child's needs as the focus.
- Maintain written record of decisions.
- Listen to feedback.
- Anticipate questions and identify alternative solutions.
- See the evaluation stage as an opportunity to learn.

8 Recording contact

As a worker with statutory responsibilities, it is important that you keep accurate records. Remember, that for auditing and inspection purposes, 'if it is not recorded, it doesn't exist'. This chapter looks at the purpose and process of recording information about contact in relation to each looked-after child.

PURPOSE OF RECORDING

Records have a variety of functions. These include the following:

- *Demonstrating accountability and compliance*: As the worker responsible for managing the contact arrangements, contact records are a means of demonstrating that your work complies with the agency's procedures and that you have fulfilled your statutory obligations. For example, that you followed through on decisions from the review or complied with the direction of court.
- *Providing evidence for decisions*: Decisions in relation to contact are open to scrutiny by your organization and also from other agencies and individuals such as the courts, the Guardian ad Litem, or the family. Contact records can provide evidence to support the actions and the decisions you have made in relation to contact. They can also be used to support decisions about other areas of the child's life, such as the potential for re-unification or the suitability of kinship care. Evidence from contact records may also be used to support decisions about future contact arrangements. For example, recorded concerns about safeguarding or patterns of attendance may inform decisions

about the type and frequency of future contact arrangements and/or determine the level of supervision required.

■ *Measuring progress against agreed objectives*: Contact records can be a means of assessing progress towards the overall aim of the care plan. For example, if the plan is for a phased return home, the behaviour of children and families during direct contact will enable workers to evaluate the frequency and length of future contact in order to prepare them for this transition.

■ *Evaluating practice*: As we saw in Chapter 7, the act of recording provides an opportunity for you to reflect upon your practice and evaluate the contact arrangements as you go along.

■ *Evidencing the resources required*: Setting up and managing contact uses a lot of resources and in these cash-strapped times, the costs associated with contact are under increasing scrutiny from managers. Keeping accurate records, such as the time and costs associated with transport, activities and supervising direct contact, can provide evidence to support any application for additional resources that are required to facilitate contact, say, assistance from contact worker or family centre.

■ *Means of sharing information*: Sharing contact records can be a way of sharing information with the family, within teams and across agencies. Sharing records with families enables them to see what is being recorded and provides an opportunity for them to record alternative views.

Reminder Box: Recording and Communicating

Shared recording systems may enable other team members and workers from other agencies to access information about contact, but remember that recording is not the same as communicating. Do not assume that information has been passed on just because you have recorded it. Make sure that essential information, such as threats to abduct a child, or changes of address are disseminated in line with your agency's procedures and that you document that this information has been shared.

In summary, there a number of reasons to keep records of contact and being aware of these will assist you to focus on particular areas of your work. The next section will go on to look at how these records are maintained.

PROCESS OF RECORDING

Methods of record keeping must comply with the policies and procedures of your agency but you may find it helpful to ask yourself the following questions.

Who Is Involved?

The method of record keeping will depend upon the purpose of the contact and the role of the person recording. We all behave differently when we know we are being observed and the presence of any worker during contact should be explained to the family from the start. For example, a Guardian ad Litem observing direct contact in order to make a recommendation to court may sit close to the family and make detailed contemporaneous records during the visit. In another situation, a foster carer facilitating unsupervised contact between siblings may be in another room during the contact visit and record only the date and time of the visit.

Reminder Box: Communicate the Purpose and Method of Recording

If you are asking a colleague, for example, a residential or contact worker, to keep records in relation to contact, you should ensure that they understand the purpose and method of recording. It is your responsibility to the allocated worker to co-ordinate the information about contact and to ensure that the mechanisms for recording it on the case file comply with statutory requirements and the policies and procedures of your agency.

How Should I Record Contact?

Before you start, think about how it feels to have things recorded about you that you can't see or challenge. Make sure that you are clear about the purpose and most appropriate method of recording. This will help you work in a more open way with children and families and will also help you to explain the process to those involved. Adopt a transparent approach.

It is good practice to share contact records wherever possible and provide information about who can access the records and where they will be kept.

Good Practice Point: Looking over Your Shoulder

Records can often reveal a lot about the values of the record keeper! If you cannot share your records as you go along, imagine that the person being written about was reading it over your shoulder.

Using the Best Tool for the Job

In practice, many agencies use pro-formas to record information about contact. These can focus on particular areas and can be a useful way to gather specific information in a consistent way. On the other hand, a standardized format can be restrictive. You may consider adapting the document to gather information that is relevant.

Use Non-Written Records

Every picture tells a story, so before reaching for the pro-formas, consider keeping non-written records of contact. Labelled photographs, videos and drawings can be a useful means of recording information visually.

Think About What Should Be Recorded

■ *Quantity and quality*: As we have seen, the quantity and quality of the record depend on the type and purpose of contact. If the purpose of direct contact is to assess the relationship between siblings in order to inform an assessment for court, then the records will include detailed qualitative information. In other cases, such as where there is regular indirect contact, your records may be more quantitative and less detailed.

■ *Fact and opinion*: Contact records should distinguish between fact and opinion.

Example from Practice: Timekeeping

Mary phoned the family centre at 2.05 p.m. to say she would be a few minutes late for her contact visit with Joe. I agreed to wait for another ten minutes. Mary arrived at 2.15 p.m. She smelled of alcohol, was unsteady on her feet and her speech was loud and slurred. In my opinion, she had been drinking. Joe appeared to be upset by Mary's appearance. He hid behind the chair and did not respond when she attempted to attract his attention through the window.

Strengths and Weaknesses

Acknowledging the things that work well and those that do not will assist you to work openly to monitor the progress made towards meeting the short- and long-term goals of contact. Addressing concerns as they arise and recording information about contacts that did happen (as well as the reasons for those that did not) provide a more complete record of contact.

Example from Practice: Addressing Concerns

I spoke with Mary in an adjacent room and asked her why she was late for the visit. She said that she had met someone on the way, had been for a couple of drinks and missed the bus. I reminded Mary that she had broken the terms of the contact agreement and, because she had been drinking, today's visit would not continue as planned.

Example from Practice: Acknowledging Strengths

Leon arrived at the park early. He had brought food for the picnic and helped the children make sandwiches. After lunch he played football with Annie and Sam. Afterwards, we talked about how the contact had gone. Leon and the children said that they enjoyed the visit and would like to have more activities like this in future.

Think about the Language Used

Case files are a key source of historical information about young people, so avoid using colloquialisms, slang or abbreviations that may not be understood in the future. Records need to be unambiguous and accurate. Make sure that they are signed and dated and that professionals are clearly identified by name and role. Ensure that all changes of name are recorded, for example, if a parent remarries or a child is adopted, so that in future, links can be made to information in other files.

Provide a Balanced Account

It is common for allegations and counter-allegations to be made during contact. Your recording should reflect the accounts of all those involved. Try to be objective and report on what happened without making judgements.

WHERE IS THE CONTACT RECORD?

Information about the contact arrangements are likely to be recorded in different parts of the child's case file, for example, in the placement plan, the care plan or in court reports. The record of the actual contact may be recorded in another part of the child's case file, for example, in the case notes, in life story work. Records may also be kept in other places, such as files in residential units, foster carer's logs.

Remember to keep a separate record for each looked-after child, even when they are placed together, and ensure that you record where other information about contact can be found, such as in a sibling's or parent's file.

In order to access quantitative information quickly, use a chronology or timetable of visits so you can access key information at a glance rather than wading through pages of contact records.

SUMMARY

In practice, many case files for looked-after children contain hundreds of pages of contact records. Remember that your records may be accessed by that child or people unfamiliar with the family years after you have written them. In summary, contact records should be:

- up to date
- legible
- accurate
- accessible
- attributable
- balanced
- quantifiable
- signed and dated
- able to identify family and workers clearly
- clearly linked to other contact records.

Further reading and resources

In practice, you may need more detailed information about specific aspects of setting up and managing contact. This chapter identifies online resources, practice guidance and further reading that you may find helpful.

LEGISLATION AND STATUTORY GUIDELINES

Most legislation and statutory guidelines are available online. The following websites contain a comprehensive range of documents and resources that may help to inform contact arrangements.

- Department for Education website – www.education.gov.uk: Publishes a range of policy, practice guidance, statutory guidance and government papers regarding children, young people and education.
- Department of Health website – www.dh.gov.uk: Publishes a range of policy, codes of practice, consultation documents and government papers of the full range of health and social care issues.
- Legislation Online – www.legislation.gov.uk. Publishes Acts of Parliament, statutory instruments and ministerial orders across the UK.

PRACTICE GUIDANCE

**Reminder Box:
Local Authorities' and
Voluntary Agencies' Webpages**

Check what resources are currently used in-house. Most statutory and voluntary organizations have their own guidance in relation to setting up and managing contact.

The following sources contain a wide range of information, news, resources and research information.

The British Association for Adoption and Fostering (BAAF)

The British Association for Adoption and Fostering (BAAF) is a UK-wide membership organization that promotes child-centred policies and services for children separated from their families of origin: www.baaf.org.uk/newadoptionandfosteringregulation.

BJSW

The British Journal of Social Work (*BJSW*). Published eight times a year, by BASW, this journal offers critical commentary on social work practice, research and theory, book reviews and a range of perspectives, including international contributions.

CAFCASS

The Children and Family Court Advisory and Support Service (CAFCASS) is a non-departmental public body which represents the interests of children involved in family proceedings. CAFCASS advises the family courts in England on what it considers to be in the best interests of individual children: www.cafcass.gov.uk.

Community Care

Community Care: www.communitycare.co.uk.This website is an easily accessible resource. It includes:

- short articles;
- updates of research;
- practice forums;
- links to discussion forums in relation to practice issues.

Specific forums for children's practice can be found on *CareSpace*: http://www.communitycare.co.uk/carespace/forums/default.aspx.

NCB

The National Children's Bureau (NCB) research centre undertakes research and work from an evidence-based perspective: www.ncb.org. uk. *Children & Society* and *Children & Young People Now* are a journal and a magazine published in association with the NCB.

Social Care Online SCIE

www.scie-socialcareonline.org.uk. Social Care Online is a database of information and research that covers all aspects of social care and social work. Resources include:

- legislation;
- government documents;
- practice and guidance;
- systematic reviews;
- research briefings;
- reports;

- journal articles;
- websites.

Every resource listed includes an abstract. Links to full text are also included where available. Social Care Online is a useful resource for those working in social work and social care.

Reminder Box: SCIE Athens

SCIE Athens service provides free access to particular social care and health journals and databases. Many employers subscribe to an Athens account which increases the amount of full-text content available through Social Care Online.

PROFESSIONAL BODIES AND STANDARDS

Professional practice is governed by codes and standards which will impact upon contact arrangements for looked-after children.

The British Association of Social Work (BASW)

The British Association of Social Work (BASW) is the largest professional association for social workers in the UK. Their website contains various resources including publications, articles and useful links: www.basw.co.uk.

The College of Social Work (TCSW)

The College of Social Work (TCSW) is the new professional body for social workers that holds the new professional standards for England, alongside the Health Care Professionals Council, who are responsible for the registration and regulation of social workers in England: www. collegeofsocialwork.org.

The Health and Care Professions Council (HCPC)

The Health and Care Professions Council (HCPC) was introduced in August 2012. It replaces the General Social Care Council (GSCC). All health, psychological and social work professionals are required to be registered with the HCPC. This means that individual professionals must meet the standard of proficiency relevant to their area of practice and also comply with the overarching standards of conduct, performance and ethics that apply to all of the 16 health and care professions regulated by the HCPC: www.hpc-uk.org.

Reminder Box: Continuing Professional Development and Registration with the HCPC

Continuing professional development (or CPD) is the way professionals keep learning and developing throughout their careers. CPD helps to keep your skills and knowledge current and encourages you to practise safely, legally and effectively. All health, psychological and social work professionals must undertake CPD to stay registered with the HCPC.

The International Federation of Social Workers (IFSW)

The International Federation of Social Workers (IFSW) is a global organization which promotes social work, best practice models and the facilitation of international co-operation. Its website allows you to access material on a range of international social work topics including policies, statements and publications on international social work: www.ifsw.org.

FURTHER READING

The following include some helpful suggestions in relation to setting up and managing contact.

Bond, H. (2007) *Ten Top Tips for Managing Contact*, London: British Association for Adoption and Fostering.

Brayne, H. and Carr, H. (2010) *Law for Social Workers*, Maidenhead: Open University Press.

British Association for Adoption and Fostering (BAAF) (2012) *New Fostering and Adoption Regulations, Guidance and National Minimum Standards*, available at: www.baaf.org.uk/newadoptionandfosteringregulation.

Department for Education (2011) *National Minimum Standards*, available at: www.education.gov.uk/publications (accessed 5 June 2012).

Department of Health (1998) *Quality Protects: Framework for Action*, London, Department of Health.

Forrester, D. (2010) The argument for evidence-based practice in social work, *Community Care*, 22 June.

Gilligan, R. (2001) *Promoting Resilience: A Resource Guide on Working with Children in the Care System*, London: British Agencies for Adoption and Fostering.

Glaser, D. (2000) Child abuse and neglect and the brain: a review, *Journal of Child Psychology and Psychiatry and Allied Disciplines*, 41(1): 97–116.

Hartman, A. and Reid, J. (1984) *Family-Centered Social Work Practice*, New York: Free Press.

Hess, P. and Proch, K. (2011) *Contact: Managing Visits to Children Looked After Away from Home*, London: British Association for Adoption and Fostering.

HM Government (2010) *The Children Act 1989: Guidance*, Volume 2: *Care Planning, Placement and Case Review*, available at: www.education.gov.uk (accessed 3 May 2012).

HM Government (2011a) *The Children Act 1989: Guidance*, Volume 4: *Fostering Services*, available at: www.education.gov.uk (accessed 3 May 2012).

H M Government (2011b) *The Children Act 1989 Guidance and Regulations,* Volume 5: *Children's Homes,* available at: www.education.gov.uk (accessed 3 May 2012).

IRO Handbook (2011) *Statutory Guidance for Independent Reviewing Officers and Local Authorities on their Functions in Relation to Case Management and Review for Looked After Children,* London: The Department for Education.

Key, T. and Scott, S. (2007) Audit of contact for Kirklees Looked After Children Team, unpublished leaflet.

Macaskill, C. (2002) *Safe Contact? Children in Permanent Placement and Contact with Their Birth Relatives,* London: Russell House Publishing.

McGoldrick, M., Gersen, R. and Shellenberger, S. (1999) *Genograms: Assessment and Intervention,* New York: W. W. Norton.

Neil, E. and Howe, D. (2010) *Contact in Adoption and Permanent Foster Care: Research, Theory and Practice,* London: BAAF.

Oxfordshire County Council Contact Planning and Information Pack, Margaret Bryer, available at: oxfordshirechildcare.proceduresonline.com/. . ./p_cont_plan_info.htm.

References

Argent, H. (ed.) (1995) *See You Soon: Contact with Children Looked After by Local Authorities,* London: BAAF.

British Association for Adoption and Fostering (BAAF) (2011) Available at: http://www.baaf.org.uk/res/statengland (accessed 23 July 2010).

Department for Education (2010) *The Children Act 1989: Guidance and Regulations,* Volume 2: *Care Planning, Placement and Case Review: The Care Planning, Placement and Case Review (England) Regulations 2010,* London: DfE.

Department for Education (2011) *The Munro Review of Child Protection: Final Report: A Child-Centred System.* London: DfE.

Department of Health (2000) *Framework for the Assessment of Children in Need and Their Families,* London: The Stationery Office.

Department of Health (2002) *Fostering Services National Minimum Standards, Fostering Services Regulations,* London: The Stationery Office.

Glaser, D. (2000) Child abuse and neglect and the brain: a review, *Journal of Child Psychology and Psychiatry and Allied Disciplines,* 41(1): 97–116.

Luft, J. and Ingham, H. (1950) The Johari window: a graphic model of interpersonal awareness. In *Proceedings of the Western Training Laboratory in Group Development,* Los Angeles: UCLA.

Neil, E. and Howe, D. (2010) *Contact in Adoption and Permanent Foster Care: Research, Theory and Practice,* London: BAAF.

Schön, D. A. (1983) *The Reflective Practitioner: How Professionals Think in Action,* London: Temple Smith.

Stein, M. (2009) *Quality Matters in Children's Services: Messages from Research,* London: Jessica Kingsley Publishers.

US Department of Defense (2002) Press release, 12 February 2002, available at: http;//www.defense.gov/transcripts/transcript.aspx?transcriptid=2636.

LEGISLATION

Adoption and Children Act 2002.
The Children Act 1989.
Children and Young Persons Act 2008.
The UK National Standards for Foster Care (1999).

Index